ELEMENTARY
ACCOUNTING

About the Authors

Royal D. M. Bauer received a Master of Business Administration degree from Northwestern University. Since 1941 he has been professor of accounting at the University of Missouri. Prof. Bauer is a Certified Public Accountant and a member of many professional organizations. In addition to *Elementary Accounting* he has had numerous articles published and is co-author of *Auditing*.

Paul Holland Darby received a Master of Arts degree from the University of Missouri. He has taught at Christian College, Kemper Military School, and Central College, all of which are located in Missouri. A Certified Public Accountant, Mr. Darby has had extensive experience in his field.

COLLEGE OUTLINE SERIES

ELEMENTARY ACCOUNTING

THIRD EDITION

by ROYAL D. M. BAUER, C.P.A.
Professor of Accounting
University of Missouri

PAUL HOLLAND DARBY, C.P.A.

BARNES & NOBLE, Inc. • NEW YORK

PUBLISHERS • BOOKSELLERS • FOUNDED 1873

Preface

The purpose of this outline is to present to the reader the principles underlying modern accounting procedures in a brief, yet reasonably comprehensive, manner.

This book is intended to meet the needs of several groups of persons, as follows:

1. Business and professional persons who need more information about accounting fundamentals.

2. Accountants and bookkeepers who wish to have a concise elementary book available for occasional reference.

3. Students who want a preliminary survey of specific materials, a constant aid to study, and a review of the elements of accounting previously studied.

4. All others who desire to increase their understanding of the methods employed to record business transactions.

The reader should bear in mind that variations are possible and even desirable in many accounting procedures, and that an adequate presentation of the subject cannot be confined to one simplified method of approach. Therefore alternative methods and synonymous terms are included in this book where necessary.

Royal D. M. Bauer
Paul H. Darby

Preface

The purpose of this volume is to present to the reader the essentials, including the basic accounting procedures, in as brief yet reasonably comprehensive a manner.

This book is intended to meet the needs of several groups of persons as follows:

1. Business and professional persons who need a one(?) information about accounting fundamentals.

2. Accountants and bookkeepers who wish to have a convenient reference book ... or utility for occasional reference.

3. Students who want a preliminary survey of another material, a general aid to study, and a review of the elements of accounting increasing needs(?).

4. Office managers who ... exercise their understanding of the methods employed in present business(?) systems.

The books should have practical ... conditions are presenting and it is desirable to have accounting procedures, and that an answers given some of the subject could be only ... be on a uniform method of approach. Therefore illustrative methods and typographical aids are provided to simplify when necessary.

ROYAL D. M. BAUER
Pacific, Iowa

Table of Contents

vii

TABULATED BIBLIOGRAPHY
OF STANDARD TEXTBOOKS

The following list gives the author, title, date, and publisher of the standard textbooks referred to in the tables on the succeeding pages.

Amory, Robert and Hardee, Covington. *Materials on Accounting*, 3rd ed., 1959, by Herwitz and Trautman, Foundation Press.

Boyd, Ralph L. and Dickey, Robert L. *Basic Accounting*, 1949, Rinehart.

Committee on Accounting, *Principles of Accounting*, 1959, Pitman.

Finney, Harry A. and Miller, Herbert E. *Principles of Accounting, Introductory*, 5th ed., 1957, Prentice-Hall.

Heckert, J. Brooks and Kerrigan, Harry D. *Accounting Systems*, 2nd ed., 1953, Ronald.

Hill, Thomas M. and Gordon, Myron J. *Accounting, a Management Approach*, rev. ed., 1959, Irwin.

Himmelblau, David. *First Year in Accounting, Fundmanetals*, 4th ed., 1952, Ronald.

Holmes, Arthur W. *et al. Elementary Accounting*, rev. ed., 1956, Irwin.

Jackson, Paul R. *Elementary College Accounting*, 1949, Prentice-Hall.

Johnson, Arnold W. *Elementary Accounting*, 4th ed., 1962, Holt, Rinehart and Winston.

Kennedy, Ralph D. and Kurtz, Frederick C. *Introductory Accounting*, 1960, International Textbook Company.

MacFarland, George A. and Ayars, Robert D. *Accounting Fundamentals*, 3rd ed., 1957, McGraw-Hill.

Mackenzie, Donald H. *The Fundmentals of Accounting*, rev. ed., 1956, Macmillan.

Mason, Perry; Davidson, Sidney; and Schindler, James S. *Fundamentals of Accounting*, 4th ed., 1959, Holt.

Mason, Perry; Stenberg, George B.; and Niven, William. *Elementary Accounting*, 2nd ed., 1956, Holt.

Meigs, Walter B. and Johnson, Charles E. *Accounting*, 1962, McGraw-Hill.

Milroy, Robert R. and Walden, Robert E.   *Accounting Theory and Practice: Introductory*, 1960, Houghton Mifflin.

Noble, Howard S. and Niswonger, Clifford R.   *Accounting Principles*, 8th ed., 1961, South-Western.

Pace, Homer St. Clair and Koestler, Edward J.   *Basic Accounting —Part I*, 1959, Pace & Pace.

———— *Basic Accounting—Part II*, 1960, Pace & Pace.

Paton, William A. and Dixon, Robert L.   *Essentials of Accounting*, 1958, Macmillan.

Pyle, William W. and White, John Arch.   *Fundamental Accounting Principles*, rev. ed., 1959, Irwin.

Schmidt, Leo A. and Bergstrom, William N.   *Fundamental Accounting*, 1952, Irwin.

Sherwood, John F. *et al.*   *College Accounting*, 6th ed., 1957, South-Western.

Tunick, Stanley B. and Saxe, Emmanuel.   *Fundamental Accounting, Theory and Practice*, 2nd ed., 1956, Prentice-Hall.

Vance, Lawrence L.   *Accounting Principles and Control*, 1960, Holt, Rinehart and Winston.

Wade, Harry W.   *Fundamentals of Accounting*, 3rd ed., 1951, Wiley.

Wixon, Rufus and Cox, Robert G.   *Principles of Accounting*, 1961, Ronald.

Quick Reference Table

All figures refer

CHAP. IN THIS BOOK	TOPIC	AMORY & HARDEE	BOYD & DICKEY	COMMIT- TEE	FINNEY & MILLER	HECKERT & KER- RIGAN	HILL & GORDON
I	Meaning and Purpose of Accounting	431-452	2-12	1-15	1-3	3-12	3-19
II	The Balance Sheet	45-48	49-65	14-26	4-10		20-50
III	The Profit and Loss Statement	9-15	14-40	27-37	22-29 68-69 362-368		50-76
IV	Accounts and the Ledger	1-15	88-98		11-15 19-91 106-111 132-139	61-81	77-106
V	The Journal and Book-keeping Procedures	24-32	130-149 160-175	38-57	15-19	82-110	27-31
VI	Periodic Adjustments and Summarization	15-42 89-211 237-303	99-128 178-206 456-498	58-74 122-224	29-76 271-285	467-476	51-94 194-209
VII	Division of the Basic Books		114-159 208-222	75-122	139-152	113-272	77-87
VIII	Auxiliary Records		130-143 224-237	157-160	126-127 235-256	275-364 479-530	80-87
IX	The Voucher System		237-244	225-246	214-234	573-620	81-82
X	Single Proprietorship-Partnership		66-68	268-305	153-174		25-36
XI	Corporation	43-45 324-370	68-85	306-360	175-214		49-50
XII	Bonds—Funds—Reserves	128-134 304-323	72-73 504-512	361-371	309-323		155-171 255-270
XIII	Industrial Accounting	393-430	41-48 193-196 326-428	406-477	338-354	623-639	107-138
XIV	Accounting for Departments, Branches, and Subsidiaries	82-88 371-392		478-509	424-437 447-450 453-463	533-570	279-287
XV	Advanced Discussion of Accounts		35-56 74 486-491	95-101 150-153 208-209	438-447		141-485
XVI	Accounting and Management		247-324 430-453	510-590	369-382 405-423		339-368 450-476

See page viii-ix for

To Standard Textbooks

to pages

HIMMEL-BLAU	HOLMES et al.	JACKSON	JOHNSON	KENNEDY & KURTZ	MACFARLAND & AYARS	MAC-KENZIE	MASON et al. FUND
1-2	1-3	1	1-12	1-5	1-8	1-9	1-18
2-5 58-59 145-149	3-11 150-164 655-665	2 34-38 237-240	13-36 72 709-718	6-20 120-121 660-671	9-23	28-46 288-303	19-39 96-97 641-648
5-6 60-62 150-156	11-17 74-93 592-599	35 232-237	52-68 218-244 661-708	21-38 120 666-670	24-39	10-27 304-323	86-97 340-347 649-654
6-13 21-22 24-26 41-49	18-40 49-51 509-514	1-27	37-51 69-72	39-69 162-172	40-49 52-64	47-91	40-60 155-173
22-24 26-32	41-49 80-84	28-31	44-47	46-49	68-83	168-174	121-143
55-58 129-138 163-175 219-232	52-150 193-203 214-237 517-583	31-44 160-231	73-120 206-214 272-352 574-638	70-151 482-550	87-133 190-206 241-252	92-167 262-287 309-312 324-370	97-99 143-154 251-391 483-531
76-83 97-100 199-208	238-287 585-589	60-80	121-205	173-241	135-152	174-177 192-261	126-188
91-95 113-122	165-213 286-295 328-345	45-59 81-128 148-159	215-218 245-271 494-513	197-241 255-269 420-481	155-168 172-186	178-185 219-227 399-401	122-123 181-196 203-217
	296-322		488-513	242-269	289-302	415-438	188-202
183-190	348-404		353-406	291-341	305-328	452-486	561-569 586-593
	405-493		407-487	342-419	330-372	487-556	569-585 593-611
	474-493	166-168 187-194	474-487 639-660	380-383 551-570	380-384 387-396	533-556 685-686	536-560 645-646
241-251	666-723		514-573	150-161 270-290 571-657	269-287	371-385 557-628 645-664	61-85 99-120 392-482
	584-625		178-205	583-587		439-451	612-637
69-76 95-97 100-102	69-79 176-184 524-535	89-93 101-102	87-120 253-260 644-652 747-759	152-162 431-443	206-210	249-250 293-295 392-399	229-259 278-279 554-557
	324-328 626-665	236-237 240-244	222-227 718-779	658-745	399-414	371-385 629-698	217-224 638-716

list of complete titles.

CHAP. IN THIS BOOK	TOPIC	MASON et al. ELEM.	MEIGS & JOHN-SON	MILROY & WALDEN	NOBLE & NIS-WONGER	PACE & KOESTLER PART I	PACE & KOESTLER PART II
I	Meaning and Purpose of Accounting	1-17	1-7	1-16	1-11	1-8	
II	The Balance Sheet	18-63 79-81 323-345	7-29 210-214 565-593	4-16 195-204 415-446	11-32 172-181 659-712	9-30 204-209	
III	The Profit and Loss Statement	64-88 177-180 321-347	59-64 215-216 688-713	25-33 196-205 416-445	33-44 171 661-709	69 212-216	
IV	Accounts and the Ledger	44-54 69-79 89-94 200-203	30-87	17-33 38-43 296-302	45-66	12-37	128-134
V	The Journal and Book-keeping Procedures	94-104	40-58	34-39 71-76	67-78	16-71	
VI	Periodic Adjustments and Summarization	81-88 110-186 271-364 414-461	71-223 293-433	39-241 349-373 390-423	90-116 163-186 229-279	170-235 245-262	1-32
VII	Division of the Basic Books	107-109 187-217	224-265	242-266 302-324 351-373	78-89 117-162	72-129 150-170	33-64 113-136
VIII	Auxiliary Records	89-94 151-170 206-270 384-400	193-206 266-292	267-295 325-348	280-304	107-120	86-112
IX	The Voucher System	400-413	619-651	460-475	305-326		65-85
X	Single Proprietorship-Partnership	9-11 563-605	434-482	476-588	401-440		137-187
XI	Corporation	10-11 508-562	483-571	589-671	441-505		188-206
XII	Bonds—Funds—Reserves	469-472 489-507	540-543 572-618	650-660	505-526	191-199	198-199
XIII	Industrial Accounting	606-688	688-762	697-722	553-619		207-223
XIV	Accounting for Departments, Branches, and Subsidiaries	690-711	652-687	432-459 773-824	527-552		60-64
XV	Advanced Discussion of Accounts	157-186 453-473	200-206 293-353 398-401 580-610	226-241 672-696	117-140 260-264 514-519	124-129	86-98
XVI	Accounting and Management	164-165 384-385 689-745	208-210 794-869	424-432 825-844	620-688		224-274

See page viii-ix for

To Standard Textbooks

to pages

PATON & DIXON	PYLE & WHITE	SCHMIDT & BERGSTROM	SHER-WOOD et al.	TUNICK & SAXE	VANCE	WADE	WIXON & COX
1-15	1-14	3-4	5-6 9-10	1-13	3-7	1-6	3-14
16-40	3-9 56-63 557-558	5-35 205-207 475-479 498-502	10-14 45-48 198-205 501-505	16-28 69 249-252 462-463	8-25 216-231 626-659	7-27	15-32 163-171 579-734
84-126	54-56 107-125 202-212	45-63 95-98 479-480 494-498	44-48 195-198 497-499	14-16 37-39 101 251-255	46-48 220-234 487-499	10-11 28-40	33-55 171-186 373-418
41-147	15-53 69-78 86-95	36-63 475-480	15-26 78-79 140-142	25-41 56-61 242-251 641-646	26-45	3-4 54-57 64-69	22-42 60-70
127-149	36-53 213-261	115-126	27-43 447-478	42-62	30-35	57-64 77-78	60-86
85-123 204-391 428-452 523-532	62-125 262-342	59-94 99-112 222-338	185-194 209-228 242-249 322-350 411-446 479-514	63-120 192-259 472-474	48-123 211-243 289-342	92-126 148-174	59-162 187-246 421-423 665-743
150-203	151-186	127-151 290-293	49-97 151-184	126-174	134-210	71-91 248-250	249-288
132-133 188-203 338-339	126-150	209-221 239-244	97-116 321-322 331, 337 351-385	103-125 175-191 260-312	139-199	133-134 142-144	87-114 265-298 570-574
392-408	343-369	152-191		313-331	249-265	127-135	289-314
9-15 558-590	400-446	341-380	289-306	332-392 466-471	393-422	1-3 192-210	10-19 228-229
11-15 591-675	447-532	383-436	307-320	393-465 471-477	423-464	1-3 211-230	11-19 635-662
667-675 694-723	533-565	317-338 407-411	255-264 439-446	437-438 446-465	344-365 447-450	182-188	619-653
409-452 496-522	566-655	290-293 439-461		478-538	507-603	231-274	345-369 449-542
533-552	187-212	388-389 479-480		514-555	467-503 626-637		379-452
204-225 453-495 552-557 676-693 724-759	140-145 236-261 552-557	172-177 239-250 313-320 394-397	150 250-255 385-410	80-97 135-171 280-309 449-465 566-572	127-165 266-288 328-336	33 153-154	91-102 380-393
744-792	656-706	172-217 465-504	205-208 497-508	313-314 556-639	606-625 655-674		543-571 593-618

list of complete titles.

How to Study Accounting

In the study of accounting, it is desirable to follow accepted procedures in order to avoid wasted effort. The following suggestions may help the student obtain the best results for the time devoted to his studies.[1]

Reading. Speed of reading, though desirable in many situations, is not stressed in the study of accounting, which requires reading for detailed information. It is well, however, to skim rapidly through a chapter for a quick overview before reading slowly for comprehension.

When reading an accounting text, it is desirable to study each example given. Answers should be found to such questions as: What was done? What was the sequence? Where did this information come from? Where did it go?

Using the Library. Most libraries have a wealth of material available, including reference books and a number of standard texts, for supplementary use with any accounting textbook. This material is usually found in the 657 section of libraries using the Dewey decimal system. Reference books may be used for further review or for intensive study of particular phases of accounting. Standard texts provide an opportunity for parallel study, so that the reader can see how different authors treat the same subject. Both reference books and textbooks are helpful when judiciously used.

Outlining and Note-Taking. By putting into his own words the author's ideas or the teacher's lectures, the student will be assisted in clarifying his own thoughts and at the same time will gain an aid for review.

Reviewing. Reviewing consists of a brief survey of the material studied. It may include the scanning of books already read, self-testing, study of notes, and the use of this *Outline*. A review is an aid to comprehension, especially if it is made accurately, carefully, and with discrimination.

Studying for periodic and final tests helps the student determine the extent of his own proficiency and discover which topics require further study.

---

[1] For a more comprehensive discussion of this subject, see *Best Methods of Study* by Samuel Smith et al., published by Barnes & Noble, Inc., New York.

Meaning and Purpose
of Accounting

NATURE OF ACCOUNTING

Records of business transactions in ancient Babylon, written in cuneiform on clay tablets over four thousand years ago, have been preserved. These tablets are the earliest known commercial records.

Present-day methods of recording business transactions are based principally on the system of bookkeeping known as double entry. Books kept according to this system for the City of Genoa in 1340 are still in existence.

The oldest significant treatise on double-entry bookkeeping now known to exist was published in Venice in 1494 by Luca Paciolo, a Franciscan monk, as part of his *Summa*, a book on mathematics.

There was little development in the subject of accounting from Paciolo's time until late in the nineteenth century. The growth of industry and commerce following the Industrial Revolution gave impetus to the development of accounting technique. Large-scale production and complexities of the modern economic structure have made necessary greatly improved accounting techniques and systems. Modern accounting in its most advanced development, however, is still based on the fundamental concepts developed by the fifteenth century.

Accounting may be defined as the mechanism and body of principles by means of which business activities that are capable of being expressed in terms of money are recorded, classified, and periodically summarized and interpreted.

BRANCHES

Accounting activities may be classified into the following branches, or fields:

1. *System building, or constructive accounting,* the planning, installation, and revision of the financial records

2. *General accounting*, including *bookkeeping* (the actual recording process) and, possibly, report preparation

3. *Cost accounting*, the determination of business costs, especially unit costs of production and distribution

4. *Auditing*, the verification of the records and preparation of reports thereon

5. *Tax accounting,* the determination of the correct liability for taxes, especially income taxes and social security taxes, and preparation of necessary returns

6. *Budgetary accounting*, the systematic forecasting of business operations in financial terms

7. *Governmental and institutional accounting*, the keeping of financial records for governmental units and agencies and non-profit institutions, and preparation of reports.

BOOKKEEPING DISTINGUISHED
FROM ACCOUNTING

Bookkeeping is the systematic recording of business transactions in financial terms. Accounting is a more comprehensive process. Usually the study of bookkeeping emphasizes technique, while the study of accounting emphasizes theory.

PURPOSE OF ACCOUNTING

Accounting provides a record of business transactions in financial terms. Accounting records are needed by non-profit-making organizations, such as governmental units, fiduciaries, and associations operating for religious, philanthropic, or fraternal purposes, as well as by business enterprises operated for profit. Records of the financial transactions of an individual or family may be considered a necessity at times. The primary purpose of accounting for a business enterprise is to provide the management with the information needed for efficient operation of that enterprise. Accounting should also make available the financial information properly desired by governmental agencies, present and prospective creditors and investors, and the general public.

UNIVERSAL NEED FOR ACCOUNTING

Fields in Which Accounting is Needed. The use of accounting training is not restricted to those who specialize in the accounting field. Many others find a knowledge of accounting principles to be useful. It is in the following three fields that a knowledge of accounting is especially valuable.

Bookkeeping and accounting. One who plans to enter the field of accounting, either as a bookkeeper with routine duties or as an accountant with greater responsibilities, should recognize the need for accounting training.

Business management. The business executive who has a knowledge of accounting is enabled thereby to understand and study financial reports. This ability should help him to evaluate more accurately the result of past operations, and to shape his future policies more intelligently.

Personal record keeping. Every person, even if he does not plan to be an accountant or a business executive, should benefit from a study of accounting. Such study should enable him to keep better personal records, to understand financial records more readily when studying them, and to be more intelligent in his spending, saving, and investing.

ACCOUNTING AND MODERN BUSINESS

Business Characteristics Leading to Accounting Development. The growth of commerce and industry has brought about the use of more adequate modern accounting records and an increasing interest in such records. Some of the features of present-day business which create a need for modern accounting methods are as follows:

1. *Size.* Business units have grown to unprecedented proportions. *Operations* are too extensive to be comprehended by an individual without summarized reports. *Information for management* must be obtained from accounting reports since personal inspection of all operations is physically impossible and verbal reports are inadequate. *Objectivity of management* enables policies to be formed without personal bias, but it cannot be maintained in a large business without comprehensive reports.

2. *Complexity of business organizations.* Operation of an enterprise has tended to become more complex under modern economic conditions, necessitating more nearly complete control through accounting.

3. *Separation of management from ownership.* The corporate form of business organization has tended to bring about the existence of managers who are not owners, and owners who do not have a direct part in running the business. Management controls the business, but stockholders control the management, and in order to do this effectively these owners must have records and reports which clearly indicate what the management has been doing.

4. *Competition.* When competition is keen, profit margins tend to become narrower. Under such conditions the information to be obtained from accurate accounting records can be especially helpful to the business management in its endeavor to reduce costs and avoid selling at a price that is economically unsound. At a time when profit margins are narrow, haphazard guessing may be disastrous.

5. *Variety of properties.* Along with the increase in the size of the business unit there has come a general diversity in the properties owned by a business. This variety of properties may be due to the increase in the number of items produced by one company, and also to the large territory which may be served by a single enterprise. *Investment and maintenance policies* relating to property often constitute a major problem in a large concern. *Depreciation policy* presents an involved problem for a business owning a variety of properties, especially if these properties have various lengths of useful life.

6. *Variety of investors.* One of the phenomena of modern business is the fact that the investment in an individual enterprise, especially the corporation, may be provided by a large number of persons. Many investors, having varying contractual relationships with the company, make accurate records necessary to disclose the status of each.

7. *Taxes and government control.* State and federal income tax laws require the exact computation of income. Other laws require periodic reports to various governmental agencies. The necessity for compliance with these laws has caused business men to see additional need for adequate records.

8. *Uniform records.* A former tendency to use accounting methods planned for the convenience of the individual firm has given way to a trend toward greater uniformity in accounting systems.

Statistics are valuable to the business man in the formation of policies. Accounts, when they are comparable, are an important source of statistical data.

Business cycles and their accompanying disorders constitute a phenomenon of the modern economic order. Studies of their causes and effects are aided by the information obtainable from uniformly kept accounts. The business cycle increases accounting problems relating to fluctuating prices and revaluation of assets.

Trade associations in some instances foster the use of uniform records and employ the information obtainable from the comparable accounts for the benefit of individual members and the industry as a whole.

Credit studies are simplified when the financial reports on which they are based, whether for obtaining credit at a bank, from another concern, or in the open market, have been prepared in such a way as to be comparable with other similar reports.

Rate making is a difficult problem. Its dependence upon uniform accounting systems is illustrated by the fact that the public utilities are required to use uniform systems established by the rate-making governmental agencies.

RELATIONSHIP OF ACCOUNTING
TO OTHER FIELDS

Viewpoint Contrasted with That of Economics. Economics ordinarily deals with society as a whole, while accounting is primarily concerned with the individual enterprise. Accounting considers gain or loss of a particular business; economics tends to disregard such variations unless they result in a net gain or loss to society.

Accounting and Engineering. Frequently problems arise that require the combined efforts of engineers and accountants. Examples may be found in the valuation of buildings and equipment, and the distribution of their cost.

Accounting and Law. Taxes, fiduciary relationships, and the formation and dissolution of partnerships and corporations give rise to some of the problems that may be solved best by the combined efforts of the accountant and the lawyer. It is desirable that the accountant know some law and that the lawyer know some accounting, but the more complex problems require expert ability in each field.

Accounting and Business Management. Accounting is a tool of management. It endeavors to keep such records as will provide the information needed or desired by the management.

ADDITIONAL BIBLIOGRAPHY*

Bauer, John, "Accounting," *Encyclopaedia of the Social Sciences,* New York: The Macmillan Co., 1930 (1937). I, 404-412.

Bolon, Dallas S., *Introduction to Accounting,* 2nd ed. New York: John Wiley & Sons, Inc., 1938. Pp. 1-6.

Cole, Dana F., *Beginning Accounting.* New York: Thomas Y. Crowell Co., 1940. Pp. 1-4.

Elwell, Fayette H., *Elementary Accounting.* Boston: Ginn and Co., 1945. Pp. 3-9.

Geijsbeek, John B., *Ancient Double Entry Bookkeeping.* Denver: J. B. Geijsbeek. 1914. Pp. 1-13.

Hatfield, Henry R., Sanders, Thomas H., and Burton, Norman L., *Accounting Principles and Practices.* Boston: Ginn and Co., 1940. Pp. 3-17.

Howard, Stanley E., *The A B C of Accounting,* 3rd ed. Princeton: Princeton University Press, 1938. Pp. 1-6.

Kelley, Arthur C., *Essentials of Accounting.* New York: American Book Co., 1935. Pp. 1-7.

Kennedy, Donald D., Esterly, George R., and von Minden, William J., *Introductory Accounting.* New York: The Ronald Press Co., 1942. Pp. 3-19

Lamberton, Robert A., *Fundamentals of Accounting.* New York: Longmans, Green and Co., 1942. Pp. 1-7.

Littleton, A. C., *Accounting Evolution to 1900.* New York: American Institute Publishing Co., 1933. Chapters 1, 6.

Peragallo, Edward, *Origin and Evolution of Double Entry Bookkeeping.* New York: American Institute Publishing Co., 1938. Chapters 1, 5, 8.

Prickett, Alva L., and Mikesell, R. Merrill, *Principles of Accounting,* rev. ed. New York: The Macmillan Co., 1937. Pp. 1-2.

Rorem, C. Rufus, and Kerrigan, Harry D., *Accounting Method,* 3rd ed.. New York: McGraw-Hill Book Co., Inc., 1942. Pp. 3-15.

Scovill, Hiram T., and Moyer, C. A., *Fundamentals of Accounting.* Boston: D. C. Heath and Co., 1940. Pp. 1-10, 761-763.

---

* For other references, see the QUICK REFERENCE TABLE TO STANDARD TEXTBOOKS in the forepart of this book.

II

The Balance Sheet

THE BALANCE SHEET EQUATION

Assets=liabilities+proprietorship. This is the fundamental balance sheet equation. It shows the equality or balance between property, including rights in property, and the claims of owners and others against the property. Its terms may be transposed from one side to the other as in any algebraic equation; for example, *assets—liabilities=proprietorship*. When either the term *liabilities* or the term *equities* is used to include both liabilities and proprietorship, the balance sheet equation becomes *assets=liabilities,* or *assets=equities.*

This equation in any of its forms shows merely that assets and the claims against them are equal in value. The claims are of two kinds, those of outside creditors, and those of the owner or owners. Outside creditors' claims are contractual, while those of the owners are residual in nature.

ASSETS, LIABILITIES, AND PROPRIETORSHIP

Assets may be defined simply as anything of value owned. They consist of rights in property and of property itself, tangible or intangible, applicable or subject to the payment of debts.

Liabilities are debts. They consist of obligations to pay money or other assets, or to render services, to another

8

person or persons either now or in the future. The term liabilities sometimes is used in a broad sense to include all claims against the assets.

Proprietorship is the excess of assets over liabilities. It is the owner's equity.[1] It represents the ownership of one or more persons who have invested more or less permanently in an enterprise and are primarily responsible for its success.

Equities are all claims against, or rights in, assets. The term thus includes liabilities to creditors and the proprietorship claims of owners.

THE STATEMENT

A *balance sheet* is a statement of the financial condition of an individual or enterprise at a given date.[2] It enumerates the amounts and the nature of the assets liabilities, and proprietorship, and is an elaboration of the equation, assets =liabilities+proprietorship. It is generally conceded to be the most important financial statement, the goal of accounting activity.

A statement of financial condition does not necessarily follow an orthodox form. However, there are two standard forms generally employed: the *account form*, or *horizontal form*, and the *report form*, or *vertical form*.

1. *Account form.*[3] This is prepared by placing the assets on the left side of the page, and the liabilities and proprietorship on the right in parallel vertical columns with equal totals. It is developed from the equation, assets=liabilities+proprietorship.

2. *Report form.* This is prepared by listing first the assets, and below them the liabilities followed by the proprietorship. One variation of the report form adds

---

1 The proprietor's equity is called variously proprietorship, capital, or net worth.
2 The balance sheet is occasionally given other titles, such as the following: financial statement; statement of financial condition; statement of assets and liabilities; statement of resources and liabilities; statement of worth; general balance sheet; and statement of assets, liabilities, and capital.
3 See Appendix A, pages 196 and 197.

liabilities and proprietorship, their total being the same as the total assets. Another variation deducts liabilities from assets, the difference being proprietorship. The first variation emphasizes the equality of assets and equities, as does the account form, and is based on the same form of equation, assets⁼liabilities+proprietorship. The second variation emphasizes the amount of proprietorship, and is based on the form of the equation, assets—liabilities⁼proprietorship.

CLASSIFICATION OF ASSETS AND LIABILITIES

Assets and liabilities may be presented on the balance sheet in classified groups in order to make them more readily understandable. Two orders of presentation are commonly found in business, one placing the current groups before the fixed, and the other placing the fixed groups before the current. The latter arrangement was widely used at one time, but the present tendency is to place the current groups first.

Current Assets consist of cash available for current use and other assets which may be sold, converted into cash, or consumed, by normal operations in the near future.[4] They are composed of items which are constantly changing, and vary in volume with the changing volume of business. This concept of current assets includes prepaid expenses.

Prepaid Expenses consist of goods or services which have been acquired for use in the business and which, in the near future, in the ordinary course of operations, will be consumed.[5] They are treated as part of the current assets

---

4 Current assets are known by a variety of terms having approximately the same meaning, such as the following: current, liquid, quick, active, turnover, circulating, and floating assets.

5 Prepaid expenses are known variously by such titles as the following: deferred charges, deferred charges to operations, deferred charges to expense, prepaid expenses, deferred expenses, and deferred assets. The titles containing the words *deferred charges* may have a broader meaning than *prepaid expenses*, for they may include such additional items as discount on bonds payable.

by many authorities. Others place them under a separate caption between the current and fixed groups. Still others place them as the last class of assets.

Fixed Assets are assets whose expected usefulness to the business will extend over several years.[6] They are more or less permanent in nature, but not necessarily immovable, and do not vary in amount with small fluctuations in the volume of business. They were not purchased for resale and will not be sold, ordinarily, so long as they serve the needs of the business. Their absence would necessitate alteration of business policies. They would be difficult to convert into cash quickly, as for the payment of debts. They are not consumed entirely in one business operation, but as in the case of buildings, machinery, and other equipment, they wear out gradually. Both tangible and intangible assets may be included among the fixed assets, but some authorities place the intangibles in a separate group. Occasionally, intangibles and miscellaneous types of assets appear together under the caption *other assets*.

Current Liabilities are liabilities which mature within a short time after they are contracted, usually a year.[7] They may include long-term liabilities becoming due within a year of the date of the balance sheet. They are payable, theoretically, out of current assets.

Income Received in Advance represents income received in one period but applicable to a subsequent period.[8] It is treated as a current liability by some authorities, and by others is given a separate classification and placed either

---

6 Fixed assets are known by various terms, such as fixed, capital, permanent, and passive assets.

7 Current liabilities are referred to by such titles as current liabilities, floating liabilities, quick liabilities, and floating debt.

8 Income received in advance is known by such terms as the following: deferred credits to income, deferred credits, deferred income, deferred liabilities, deferred revenue, prepaid income, and income received in advance. The term deferred credits has a broader meaning than the other terms here used when it includes deferred credits to expense, such as premium received on bonds payable. Under such circumstances some authorities treat deferred credits as fixed liabilities.

between current and fixed liabilities or as the last group of liabilities.

Fixed Liabilities are liabilities that will not mature for a comparatively long time, usually more than a year.[9]

CHANGES IN BALANCE SHEET ITEMS

Transactions of a business cause increases and decreases in its assets, liabilities, and proprietorship.

Asset Changes. Assets are constantly changing through (1) purchases or other acquisition, (2) fabrication in the manufacturing process, (3) conversion, (4) depreciation, and (5) sales or other disposition.

Liability Changes. Liabilities are constantly changing through (1) additional purchases on credit, (2) borrowing, (3) paying off liabilities, and (4) exchanging one liability for another.

Proprietorship Changes. The proprietary interest is constantly changing through (1) additional investments in the business, (2) profit or loss from operations, (3) gain or loss on non-operating activities, and (4) withdrawals of earnings and of investments.

ADDITIONAL BIBLIOGRAPHY*

Bolon, Dallas S., *Introduction to Accounting*, 2nd ed. New York: John Wiley & Sons, Inc., 1938. Pp. 7-19, 38-39, 252-256.

Cole, Dana F., *Beginning Accounting*. New York: Thomas Y. Crowell Co., 1940. Pp. 5-41, 68-80, 384-389.

Elwell, Fayette H., *Elementary Accounting*. Boston: Ginn and Co., 1945. Pp. 26-36, 97-110.

Hatfield, Henry R., Sanders, Thomas H., and Burton, Norman L., *Accounting Principles and Practices*. Boston: Ginn and Co., 1940. Pp. 18-51, 67-70, 78-80.

Howard, Stanley E., *The A B C of Accounting*, 3rd ed. Princeton: Princeton University Press, 1938. Pp. 7-33.

---

9 Fixed liabilities are also known by such terms as long-term obligations, long-term liabilities, long-term debt, and funded debt.

* For other references, see the QUICK REFERENCE TABLE TO STANDARD TEXTBOOKS in the forepart of this book.

Jackson, J. Hugh, *Accounting Principles*. Los Angeles: Charles R. Hadley Co., 1944. Pp. 9-23, 334-345.

Kelley, Arthur C., *Essentials of Accounting*. New York: American Book Co., 1935. Pp. 10-20.

Kennedy, Donald D., Esterly, George R., and von Minden, William J., *Introductory Accounting*. New York: The Ronald Press Co., 1942. Pp. 43-84.

Lamberton, Robert A., *Fundamentals of Accounting*. New York: Longmans, Green and Co., 1942. Pp. 8-25.

Prickett, Alva L., and Mikesell, R. Merrill, *Principles of Accounting*, rev. ed. New York: The Macmillan Co., 1937. Pp. 2-18.

Rorem, C. Rufus, and Kerrigan, Harry D., *Accounting Method*, 3rd ed. New York: McGraw-Hill Book Co., Inc., 1942. Pp. 16-30, 206-215, 355-461, 510-536.

Scovill, Hiram T., and Moyer, C. A., *Fundamentals of Accounting*. Boston: D. C. Heath and Co., 1940. Pp. 11-44, 242-260.

III

The Profit and Loss Statment

INCOME AND EXPENSES

Income. There are many interpretations of the meaning of income. Income may be defined as the exchange value of personal and professional services rendered or of goods sold in the primary operations of a business.[1] Primary operations relate to those transactions which constitute the principal activities of a business. Income, so defined, is gross income in the opinion of many.[2] From this gross income must be subtracted all operating costs and expenses to obtain the net operating income, or operating profit.

Non-operating income is the gain realized on the rendering of unusual services and the loan or sale of assets not needed in the primary operations of the business. Non-operating income may be more broadly defined to include all increases in proprietorship other than income from the primary operations of the business and additional investment of the owners.

---

1 Variations in the interpretations of the meaning of income give rise to three principal definitions of the term.
1. Income is the exchange value of goods or services sold. It is variously termed sales, gross sales, net sales, gross income from sales and services, gross income, revenue, gross revenue, gross receipts from operations, earnings, and gross earnings.
2. Income is the difference between sales and cost of goods sold. This, in the opinion of many, is gross margin, gross margin on sales, gross profit, or gross profit on sales.
3. Income is the increase in proprietary interest resulting from any cause other than additional investment of the owners. Some authorities refer to this as net income, net profit, net gain, or net revenue.

2 Gross income may thus be considered as net sales. Gross income is considered by some to be the difference between net sales and the cost of goods sold plus all other, or non-operating, income. This is also called income.

Expense may be defined as the cost of revenue gained, or as the exchange value of commodities and services consumed in the operation of the business.[3]

Operating expenses are expenses incurred in the primary operations of the business. *Non-operating expenses* are expenses incurred in operations other than the primary operations of the business. Some authorities consider non-operating expenses to include all decreases in proprietorship other than decreases resulting from the primary operations of the business and withdrawals of capital by the owners.

Expense is sometimes confused with the terms cost, expenditure, disbursement, outlay, outgo, and loss. In order to minimize confusion these terms should be defined.

1. *Cost* is sometimes considered to be identical in meaning with expense. Another concept of cost is that it occurs when assets or services are exchanged or debts incurred for other assets or for expenses.

2. *Expenditure* is considered by some to be the payment of money or services or the incurring of debts for any asset or expense. This is identical with one concept of the meaning of cost. A more general concept of expenditure is that it represents the payment of cash. In this sense it is synonymous with disbursement, outlay, and outgo.

3. *Disbursement, outlay,* and *outgo* are terms which refer to the payment of cash.

---

3 Usage of the term expense indicates that there are three principal concepts of its meaning.

    1. Expense is the cost of obtaining income, as defined above.

    2. Expense may be defined more narrowly as the exchange value of commodities and services, other than the cost of goods sold, consumed in the operations of the business.

    3. Expense may be defined broadly to include all items which in themselves decrease proprietorship, except capital withdrawals by the owners. This definition includes all expenses covered by the first definition and, in addition, such items as income taxes (which may be considered to be a share of the profits taken by the government) and recorded extraordinary losses due to decreases in asset values resulting from fires, storms, and market variations.

4. *Loss* is any decrease in the value of assets or any increase in liabilities for which no benefit is received by the enterprise. It is usually involuntary and irregular in occurrence. *Loss* is used also to refer to the excess of expenses over income. The term *net loss* may be used as the opposite of *net profit*. Certain items are labeled losses by some authorities, while others prefer to call them expenses. For example, ordinary losses on bad debts, consisting of debts owed to the enterprise which are not collectible, claims from customers for shortages or damages, and the customary breakage and spoilage of goods in the process of manufacturing, represent a disappearance of values without a clearly discernible return. However, the business enterprise must assume a certain amount of such risks if it extends credit to its customers, and if its manufacturing processes are to move with speed. It is customary, therefore, to consider such items as expenses because of their regular recurrence and because of their prevalence in business. If they are extraordinarily large and irregular, they may properly be labeled losses.

THE STATEMENT

A *profit and loss statement* is a statement of the incomes and expenses of an individual or enterprise for a given period.[4] It enumerates the amounts and the nature of the incomes and expenses and the amount of the difference, which is the net profit or loss for the period. This statement shows the results of operations for a period of time, while the balance sheet shows the financial condition at a given

---

4 The profit and loss statement is occasionally given other titles, such as the following: income statement; statement of income and expense; statement of income, profit, and loss; operating statement; income sheet; profit and loss account; income account; statement of loss and gain; revenue statement; statement of expense and revenue; statement of operating results; trading, profit, and loss statement; statement of income and capital account; statement of earnings; summary of income and expense; and profit and loss summary.

date. Among financial statements the profit and loss statement is generally conceded to be second in importance only to the balance sheet. However, some authorities consider it more important than the balance sheet. It is in reality a part of the proprietorship section of the balance sheet, a complementary statement, in that it shows how the proprietorship was changed as a result of the activities of the business. Some accountants omit showing changes in proprietorship of an extraordinary nature in the profit and loss statement, but place them in a separate statement. A more complete form of profit and loss statement may be prepared so as to show not only changes in proprietorship due to operating and non-operating incomes and expenses, but also such changes as are due to the withdrawal or additional investment of the proprietors. Thus the profit and loss statement becomes a complete analysis of the proprietorship changes for the period covered.

Like the balance sheet, the profit and loss statement is not necessarily prepared according to a standard form. Two general types of forms are commonly employed, however. They are the *account form*, sometimes called the *horizontal form*, and the *report form*, sometimes called the *vertical form*, or *narrative form*.

1. *Account form.* This is prepared by placing the cost of goods sold and expenses on the left side of the page and the incomes on the right, using parallel vertical columns. Equal totals are obtained by the balancing process. If it is desired to show cost of goods sold in more detail, the opening inventories and purchases may be shown on the left side among the expenses and the closing inventories on the right side.

In order that types of operations may be segregated and desired sub-totals given, the various items may be classified into accounts such as the following: manufacturing, selling (trading), general and ad-

ministrative (overhead), non-operating, and perhaps
federal income tax and appropriation.

The account form of profit and loss statement is
technical. It is easily prepared by the accountant,
but not easily understood by one unacquainted with
bookkeeping techniques. It is used less frequently than
formerly, being superseded by the report form.

2.   *Report form.*[5]   In this form the items of income and
expense are segregated into sections rather than accounts. Some of the sections commonly employed in
a mercantile enterprise are as follows: sales, cost of
goods sold, operating expenses, and non-operating income and expenses. The computations which are made
are described below in the discussion of classification.

CLASSIFICATION OF PROFIT AND
LOSS STATEMENT ITEMS

In a general way the income and expense items in all
types of business are similar, but differences exist, especially
among such organizations as a mercantile business, a manufacturing concern, an enterprise which renders personal services, and an enterprise which engages in more than one of
these activities.

The classification of incomes and expenses is a relative
matter. For instance, expenses which can be classed as
operating for one concern may be non-operating expenses
for another. The following is a sectional classification of
the income and expense items relating to a mercantile company, together with various important computed totals.

Sales. This section shows the gross sales, sales returns, sales allowances, net sales, and sometimes sales discounts.

1.   *Gross sales* include the total amount customers have
paid or agreed to pay for merchandise sold during

---

5 See Appendix A, page 198.

the accounting period. This term excludes sales of assets other than merchandise held for resale.

2. *Sales returns* represent merchandise sold which for any reason has been returned.

3. *Sales allowances* are deductions from the sales price to customers in lieu of the return of merchandise which is unsatisfactory.

4. *Sales discounts* are special discounts allowed customers for prompt payment. They are placed in this section by some authorities.

5. *Net sales* are determined by deducting from gross sales the sales returns, sales allowances, and sales discounts if included in this section.

Cost of Goods Sold. This section shows the beginning inventory, purchases, freight and cartage in, purchase returns, purchase allowances, cost of goods available for sale, the ending inventory, cost of goods sold, and sometimes purchase discounts.

In a manufacturing enterprise the cost of goods sold section may include the above items and also such additional items as relate to the manufacturing process.

1. *Beginning inventory* represents the merchandise on hand at the beginning of the accounting period.

2. *Purchases* include the cost of merchandise acquired for resale during the accounting period. This term excludes acquisitions of assets other than merchandise purchased for resale.

3. *Freight and cartage in,* or *transportation in,* represents transportation costs of merchandise purchased for resale.

4. *Purchase returns* represent merchandise which for

any reason has been returned to the vendors, from whom it was purchased.

5. *Purchase allowances* are deductions from the purchase price obtained from vendors in lieu of the return to them of merchandise which is unsatisfactory.

6. *Purchase discounts* are special discounts received for prompt payment of invoices for merchandise purchases. They are placed in this section by some authorities.

7. *Cost of goods available for sale* is a computed total obtained by adding to the beginning inventory purchases and transportation in, and subtracting purchase returns, purchase allowances, and purchase discounts if included in this section.

8. *Ending inventory* represents the merchandise on hand at the end of the accounting period.

9. *Cost of goods sold* is a computed total obtained by subtracting the ending inventory from the cost of goods available for sale.

Gross Profit. This is a computed total obtained by subtracting cost of goods sold from net sales.[6]

Operating Expenses. This section is ordinarily subdivided into selling expenses and general and administrative expenses.

1. *Selling expenses* include all expenses directly relating to the sale of merchandise. Some of the items ordinarily found in this group are as follows: sales salaries and commissions, advertising, delivery expenses, insurance on merchandise and sales equipment, taxes and licenses applicable to sales, depreciation of

---

6 Gross profit is also called gross profit on sales, gross trading profit, gross margin on sales, gross margin, and sometimes, as previously indicated, income.

sales equipment, sales supplies used, miscellaneous selling expenses, and sometimes bad debts expense. These items may be subdivided and other items may be added.

2. *General and administrative expenses* include all operating expenses except those directly relating to the sale of merchandise. Some of the items ordinarily found in this group are as follows: office salaries, rent, telephone and telegraph, light and heat, miscellaneous taxes and licenses, insurance and depreciation not applied to sales, office supplies used, and miscellaneous office expense. Sometimes bad debts expense, sales discounts, and interest expense, are included in this section as financial management expense, which may be offset by financial management income such as purchase discounts and interest earned. Items in this group, as in the case of selling expenses, may be subdivided and other items may be added.

Operating Profit or Operating Loss. This is a computed total obtained by subtracting operating expenses from gross profit. If gross profit is greater than operating expenses, the difference is called *operating profit*. If operating expenses are greater than gross profit, the negative figure resulting is called *operating loss*.[7]

Non-operating Income and Non-operating Expenses. Non-operating income and non-operating expenses, previously defined, may include those items of income and expenses which do not result from operations for which the business was principally organized.[8]

---

7 Various additional titles used for the difference between gross profit and operating expenses are as follows: net operating profit, net profit from operations, net operating revenue, net operating income, net operating gain, net gain from operations, net operating loss, and net loss from operations.

8 The non-operating income and non-operating expenses section may also be given the following titles: other income and other expenses, outside income and outside expenses, financial and other income and expenses, and extraneous income and expenses.

1. *Non-operating income* includes such items as interest, rent, and sometimes purchase discounts and extraordinary gains.

2. *Non-operating expenses* include such items as interest and sometimes sales discounts, bad debts expense, and extraordinary expense or loss.

Net Profit or Net Loss. Net profit or net loss is a computed total obtained by taking into consideration the operating profit or loss and the non-operating income and expenses. If there is an operating profit, non-operating income will be added and non-operating expenses will be subtracted to obtain net profit or loss. If there is an operating loss, non-operating income will be subtracted and non-operating expenses will be added to obtain net profit or loss. Instead of the separate adding or subtracting of non-operating income and expenses, the difference between them may be added to or subtracted from operating profit or loss to obtain net profit or loss.

ADDITIONAL BIBLIOGRAPHY*

Bolon, Dallas S., *Introduction to Accounting*, 2nd ed. New York: John Wiley & Sons, Inc., 1938. Pp. 63-72, 262-272.

Cole, Dana F., *Beginning Accounting*. New York: Thomas Y. Crowell Co., 1940. Pp. 42-64, 130-132, 389-396.

Elwell, Fayette H., *Elementary Accounting*. Boston: Ginn and Co., 1945. Pp. 24-36, 91-97.

Hatfield, Henry R., Sanders, Thomas H., and Burton, Norman L., *Accounting Principles and Practices*. Boston: Ginn and Co., 1940. Pp. 52-66.

Howard, Stanley E., *The A B C of Accounting*, 3rd ed. Princeton: Princeton University Press, 1938. Pp. 34-51.

Jackson, J. Hugh, *Accounting Principles*. Los Angeles: Charles R. Hadley Co., 1944. Pp. 42-50, 345-354.

Kelley, Arthur C., *Essentials of Accounting*. New York: American Book Co., 1935. Pp. 21-27.

Kennedy, Donald D., Esterly, George R., and von Minden, William J., *Introductory Accounting*. New York: The Ronald Press Co., 1942. Pp. 20-42.

Lamberton, Robert A., *Fundamentals of Accounting*. New York: Longmans, Green and Co., 1942. Pp. 26-40.

---

* For other references, see the QUICK REFERENCE TABLE TO STANDARD TEXTBOOKS in the forepart of this book.

Prickett, Alva L., and Mikesell, R. Merrill, *Principles of Accounting,* rev. ed. New York: The Macmillan Co., 1937. Pp. 19-35.

Rorem, C. Rufus, and Kerrigan, Harry D., *Accounting Method,* 3rd ed. New York: McGraw-Hill Book Co., Inc., 1942. Pp. 108-118, 216-227, 463-490, 537-558.

Scovill, Hiram T., and Moyer, C. A., *Fundamentals of Accounting.* Boston: D. C. Heath and Co., 1940. Pp. 40-42, 115-124, 242-260.

Accounts and the Ledger

BUSINESS TRANSACTIONS

Dual Elements in Every Transaction. A transaction is an exchange of values. It is composed of two elements, both of which must be recorded in order to make a complete financial record. In any transaction the presence of the dual elements is evident in the fact that on one hand a commodity, right, or service is received, and on the other hand a commodity, right, or service is given up. An exchange has taken place.[1] When these elements are recorded on the books of the business negotiating the transaction, they cause increases and decreases in the assets, liabilities, and proprietorship of the business. For instance, analysis will show that if a transaction results in the increase of an asset, there will at the same time be a corresponding decrease in another asset or an increase in either liabilities or proprietorship. This is only one instance of the various ways in which the balance sheet may be affected by transactions.

Effects of Business Transactions on Financial Records. Every transaction involves only the three balance sheet elements, assets, liabilities, and proprietorship, causing increases and decreases in these elements. The effects of transactions on the financial records, therefore, consist only of asset changes, liability changes, and proprietorship

---

1 A distinction sometimes is made between an exchange and a conversion. In a conversion the dual elements of the transaction appear in the fact that a new commodity, right, or service results from the transformation of previously held commodities, rights, or services. In both an exchange and a conversion, however, one commodity, right, or service takes the place of another.

changes, or combinations thereof. Any changes in the income and expense items are basically proprietorship changes whose ultimate effects are reflected in the balance sheet.

Fundamental Types of Transactions. In terms of the balance sheet equation there are only nine fundamental types of transactions. They are as follows:

Asset increase accompanied by:

1. Asset decrease
2. Liability increase
3. Proprietorship increase

Liability decrease accompanied by:

4. Asset decrease
5. Liability increase
6. Proprietorship increase

Proprietorship decrease accompanied by:

7. Asset decrease
8. Liability increase
9. Proprietorship increase.

In actual business transactions, combinations of these fundamental types are commonly found.

PHILOSOPHY OF DEBIT AND CREDIT

It is desirable to use a system of recording business transactions which will show changes in assets, liabilities, and proprietorship with a minimum of space, effort, and error. It should be possible to give information about each transaction that will indicate clearly just what effect it has had on the balance sheet items, and then, with the least possible additional effort, there should be a more or less automatic proof of the accuracy of the resulting figures. A poor accounting system may require much unnecessary work.

Preparation of a new balance sheet from the old after each transaction would show the effect of the transaction and indicate the new total assets offset by the total amount of liabilities and proprietorship. Such a system, however, would be extremely cumbersome, especially in a large business enterprise. No business executive is likely to want a complete new balance sheet after each transaction. If such balance sheets were desired, they would not show how the changes came about, or provide the information necessary to construct the profit and loss statement. Greater efficiency is obtained by analyzing periodically the totals of some forms of transactions, such as sales, than by attempting to determine for each transaction what its full effect is on the balance sheet. Under such a system, where some analyses will be made only at intervals, a record, nevertheless, should be made promptly for each transaction.

Accounting techniques which are in use at present give a brief and accurate method of recording transactions. They separate the increases, or positive elements, from the decreases, or negative elements, relative to each account, and then require a balancing of all asset accounts against all liability and proprietorship accounts.

It is a principle of debit and credit that the elements comprising business transactions should be separated and classified and their combined results balanced, in order to produce satisfactory business records efficiently.

Accounts. As discussed later in this chapter, **accounts are a device used to record the effects of transactions on the** assets, liabilities, and proprietorship of an enterprise. A business unit will use as many accounts, ordinarily, as it deems necessary to provide the detailed information it needs. The information given by these accounts is assembled periodically in the construction of a balance sheet and a profit and loss statement, supplemented perhaps by detailed schedules.

In the interests of convenience and uniformity, a conventional method of recording the balance sheet items in the accounts has been adopted generally. This method places additions to the assets on the left side of the accounts in which they are recorded and additions to the liabilities and proprietorship items on the right side of their accounts. This is in harmony with the balance sheet arrangement which places assets on the left side and liabilities and proprietorship on the right. Then when an asset is increased as the result of a transaction, the amount of the increase is recorded in the asset account on the left side. When a liability or a proprietorship item is increased, the amount of the increase is placed in its account on the right side. Conversely, when an asset is decreased, the amount of the decrease is shown on the right side of the asset account; when a liability or a proprietorship item is decreased, the amount of the decrease is shown on the left side of the account that is affected.

In addition to the asset, liability, and proprietorship accounts, a number of temporary proprietorship accounts usually appear in the records under the classifications of income accounts and expense accounts. Income accounts have the effect of increasing proprietorship and expense accounts decrease it.

An Expanded Accounting Equation. The balance sheet equation given in Chapter II is reproduced here with the addition of income and expense accounts. This expanded accounting equation, sometimes called the financial and operating equation, illustrates with plus and minus signs the side of each class of accounts which contains increases and the side which contains decreases.

$$\text{Assets} = \text{Liabilities} + \text{Proprietorship} + \text{Income} - \text{Expense}$$

+	−	−	+	−	+	−	+	+	−

DEBIT AND CREDIT

An understanding of the method of recording requires some familiarity with the terminology used by bookkeepers and accountants. Some of the terms have been commonly accepted and used in the business world for hundreds of years, even antedating the writings of Paciolo. Two terms are used in the recording process in connection with every business transaction. They are *debit* and *credit*. Custom has given conventional meanings to these words. Debit (abbreviated *Dr.*) refers to the left side of an account and credit (abbreviated *Cr.*) refers to the right side. When used as a noun, a debit is an entry on the left side and a credit is an entry on the right side of an account. As an adjective, the debit side of an account is the left side and the credit side is the right side. As a verb, to debit is to make an entry on the left side and to credit is to make an entry on the right side of an account. The word *charge* sometimes is used instead of the word *debit*.

Remembering the debit and credit sides of an account, the increases and decreases shown in the expanded accounting equation above can be summarized as follows:

Debit indicates:	*Credit* indicates:
Asset increase	Asset decrease
Liability decrease	Liability increase
Proprietorship decrease	Proprietorship increase
Income decrease	Income increase
Expense increase	Expense decrease.

Since there is the two-fold aspect to each transaction, a complete record of a transaction requires that the total amounts of the debits and credits must be equal. This gives rise to a fundamental rule of accounting—for every debit there must be a credit. It is not necessary that there be the same number of debit and credit items, but the debit and credit *amounts* must be equal.

DOUBLE-ENTRY BOOKKEEPING

Double-entry bookkeeping is the orderly recording of business transactions in financial terms in a manner which shows the effect of each transaction on the assets, liabilities, and proprietorship, and, at the same time, maintains the equality of the total debits and credits. It is an effective and consistent system, of which an important part is the showing of the positive and negative elements relating to each item in separate columns. The double-entry system, though following established principles, has been revised to keep step with progress in modern enterprises.

ACCOUNT FORM AND CONSTRUCTION

An account may be defined as a systematic arrangement of the increases and decreases of some specific asset, liability, or proprietorship item, or subdivision thereof, expressed in financial terms, such increases and decreases usually being segregated in parallel vertical columns.[2]

Structure of the Account. In its simplest form, an account may be shown as a *skeleton* account, in order to save space and simplify the presentation of examples. The Cash account, for instance, which has a balance of $900.00 may be presented as follows:

Cash

900.00 |

This is called a *T* account, because of its resemblance to a capital letter "T." The name of the account is placed at the top on the horizontal line. The vertical line separates the debits on the left from the credits on the right. This account form does not give sufficient information for most bookkeeping purposes, however.

---

2 An account, in a broad sense, is any device for recording the accumulated increases and decreases in an asset, a liability, or net worth. This is true regardless of the form used. For instance, a check book with the stubs completed so as to show withdrawals and deposits of cash is a form of cash account.

A more nearly complete example of the T account, which is widely used, supplies columns for additional data somewhat as follows:

Cash

19....								
Jan. 1	Balance		900.00					
(1)	(2)	(3)	(4)	(1)	(2)	(3)	(4)

This type of account is known as the *standard* account form. The columns provide space for the following information: (1) date of each entry, (2) necessary description or supplementary information, (3) folio or cross reference to indicate the page in another record on which a preliminary analysis of the transaction or transactions involved appears, and (4) amount.

Another widely used account form contains the date, explanation, and folio columns but once and the debit and credit amount columns are placed side by side at the right. In addition, there may be a column or two for the balance, the difference between the amount columns.

Many other forms of accounts are used. Specialized methods of recording, as with machines, have been the cause of numerous variations. Special types of information needed about some classes of transactions may make additional columns and special forms necessary.

Footing the Accounts. When the present status of an account is desired, this is ascertained by adding all the debit items and writing the total in small pencil figures below the last line used and doing the same for the credit items. The difference between the total debits and the total credits, which is called the balance, is written in the description column of the larger side. The balance is a debit balance when the debit side is the larger, and a credit balance when the credit side is the larger.

CLASSES OF ACCOUNTS

Accounts may be grouped into six principal classes, as follows:

1. Asset accounts
2. Liability accounts
3. Proprietorship accounts
4. Summarizing accounts
5. Income accounts
6. Expense accounts.

The asset, liability, proprietorship, income, and expense accounts contain the account elements suggested by their names. A summarizing account, usually called *Profit and Loss* account, *or Profit and Loss Summary* account, is used as a clearing account to which income and expense account balances are transferred at the end of an accounting period. The result of their combined balances is then transferred to the proprietorship accounts. Sometimes one or more additional summarization accounts are used, such as a Cost of Goods Sold account and a Trading account.

There are many ways in which the accounts may be grouped, depending upon the point of view. Sometimes they are classified into the following four groups: assets, liabilities, income, and expense. When accounts are so grouped, the term liabilities is used in a broad sense to include proprietorship, and summarizing accounts are omitted. The account *elements* are then considered to be four in number, as indicated by the names of the four groups.

Real and Nominal Accounts. A convenient method of dividing the accounts into two groups is based on the financial statements. The asset, liability, and proprietorship accounts are labeled *real* accounts, and the income, expense, and summarizing accounts, *nominal* accounts.[3] The real accounts represent items which are more or less permanent. Their balances at the end of one accounting period are retained as the balances at the beginning of the next period. The nominal accounts do not continue from year to year, but are transferred to the proprietorship accounts periodically, usually as often as once a year. Such transfers seldom are made directly but are made through the summarizing account, Profit and Loss.

Mixed Accounts. At the close of an accounting period, some accounts commonly contain both real and nominal elements. These accounts are known as *mixed* accounts. The Prepaid Insurance account is an example. When a fire insurance premium is paid in advance, the amount becomes an asset representing a claim against the insurance company for the protection specified by the insurance policy. Later, a part of the prepaid insurance becomes insurance expense as the time passes that is covered by the policy. At the close of an accounting period, the amount of expired premium is recorded as an expense of the period and the unexpired portion remains as an asset.

Suspense Account. Sometimes there is not sufficient information available about a transaction to complete the record at once, or an error may be discovered in the records which can be corrected more easily at a later date. Under such circumstances a suspense account may be used in which to place the questionable item until the necessary information is obtained. Accounts receivable and notes receivable whose collectibility is doubtful are sometimes recorded in suspense accounts. A suspense account may be used at times as a convenient temporary expedient, but it should be used

---

3 Real accounts are also known as balance sheet or permanent accounts. Nominal accounts may be called profit and loss, loss and gain, temporary, temporary proprietorship, intermediate, supplementary, ancillary, economic, explanation, fictitious, or representative accounts.

sparingly, and ordinarily it should not be carried beyond the close of an accounting period.

Personal and Impersonal Accounts. A distinction may be made between personal and impersonal accounts, personal referring to accounts with persons and impersonal indicating all other accounts.

Permanent and Temporary Proprietorship Accounts. Income, expense, and summarizing accounts are in reality temporary proprietorship accounts, as already indicated. They contain information which could be recorded directly in the proprietorship accounts, but a segregation is made into individual accounts to provide an analysis of the various kinds of income and expense. At the end of an accounting period, the temporary accounts customarily are closed directly or indirectly into the proprietorship accounts.

THE LEDGER

The ledger is a group of accounts. It is a derived, or secondary, record presenting in analytical form the accumulated effects of transactions on the assets, liabilities, and proprietorship. Its sources of information are the books of original entry, called journals. Usually only one account is placed on each page of the ledger.

Business practice formerly favored the use of bound books for the accounts, but the present tendency is to use loose-leaf forms printed on paper or cards. The bound ledger is inflexible in that new accounts or additional space for old accounts must be placed where blank pages are available. The increasingly popular loose-leaf ledger is more flexible and permits rearrangement of the accounts, if necessary. Sheets may be removed readily so that entries can be made with bookkeeping machines. New accounts may be placed where desired, and additional space may be given an account merely by inserting a new sheet along with the old. Furthermore, completely filled or dead sheets may be placed in a separate binder for storage so that the current binder need not be unduly large.

CLASSIFICATION

Accounts usually are placed in a ledger and classified in some systematic manner. Even in a bound ledger it is customary to arrange the accounts in some definite order when they are first placed in the book. The order of their appearance will vary according to the needs and procedures of the business. The number of accounts will also vary, depending upon the amount of detail desired and the type of business.

Efficiency is promoted if care is used in planning the sequence of the accounts so that any desired account can be found quickly. Several methods are in general use.

Financial Statement Sequence is a popular plan for the arrangement of accounts. By placing the accounts in the ledger in the order of their appearance on the financial statements, a classification is obtained which groups the accounts according to classes and simplifies preparation of the statements. An individual account can be located quickly by remembering its position on the balance sheet or profit and loss statement, or by referring to a list or chart of the accounts.

Alphabetical Order is another arrangement which is used extensively, especially where the accounts are few in number. Each account appears in alphabetical order according to the first significant word in its title, regardless of its position on the financial statements.

Other Sequences of accounts in the ledger are varied and depend on the particular type of enterprise involved and the personnel of the accounting department. The accounts receivable may be arranged in a separate ledger according to their geographical location if the management so desires.

The accounts may be classified objectively, or according to object or nature, so that there is an account for each general class or type of object for which the enterprise desires separate information. For instance, all of the machinery may be recorded in a Machinery account, and all wages expense may appear in one Wages account. A more detailed classification may be desired, providing a record by departments or according to the functional organization of the enterprise. Such a classification by functions requires subdivision of the accounts relating to departmental activities in order that the results of operations of each department may be determined separately.

The bound ledger, once the predominating type of ledger used, does not permit the continued use of any of these preceding arrangements, except for a time after the accounts are first placed in the book. Eventually spaces allotted for certain accounts will be filled, and new accounts or additional space for existing accounts will have to be located anywhere that blank pages are available.

CODIFICATION

Number and Letter Designations. Code numbers or letters, co-ordinated with the classification system, frequently serve to designate the various accounts. In a large enterprise, which requires a complex system of records and many accounts, there is need for some symbolic method of referring to the accounts in order to avoid constant repetition of the full descriptive titles. This makes possible a saving of time and perhaps a saving of space in some of the records where a cross reference to the accounts is needed. A small business also may find such symbols desirable, but the need for them will be less urgent. Any system of codification must be planned with care to provide flexibility for normal expansion and minor changes in the classification.

Numerical Systems of identifying the accounts are widely used. By combinations of numbers the relationship between various accounts in a group may be shown. The first number or numbers may indicate the group to which an account belongs, and will be repeated for each account in that group. Subsequent figures indicate subdivisions of that group, and will be the same if the particular type of account under consideration is found in more than one general group. Thus the number *1* may refer to all assets. The number *11* may refer to the current assets, indicating that they are the first group of asset accounts, and *111* will be the code number for Cash as the first account among the current assets. If there are three cash accounts, the *111* will indicate their group location, and their individual numbers will be *111.1*, *111.2*, and *111.3*. Notes Receivable account will be numbered *112*, as the second class of accounts among the current assets. If there are two notes receivable accounts, their numbers will be *112.1* and *112.2*. When the fixed assets are listed as the second major group of assets, their group number is *12* and the first account within the group is numbered *121*. (Appendix A, page *189*.)

This indicates roughly one way in which the Dewey decimal system is applied to the coding of accounts. It affords great flexibility in the adaptation to a firm's individual needs. Other numerical systems include the simple consecutive numbering of all accounts in the order of their appearance in the ledger, and a variety of groupings of numbers.

Mnemonic Systems use code letters instead of figures to identify accounts. Key letters may indicate the groups to which accounts belong, and other letters disclose the sub-classifications within the groups. Combinations of letters and numbers may be used.

THE CHART OF ACCOUNTS

A chart showing the order in which the accounts are arranged is a convenient index to the ledger, and an aid in the preparation of the financial statements.[4] The chart of accounts can be useful in a number of ways.

1. *An aid in system installation and revision.* When one is planning the installation of a new accounting system or the revision of an old one, it is desirable throughout the planning period to give serious thought to the accounts that will be needed by the enterprise. The effectiveness of the new records may be dependent to a great extent on the proper planning of the accounts. One of the early steps will be the preparation of a tentative chart of accounts. If the accounting problems are complex, the chart may need constant attention and numerous revisions before plans for the new records are completed. The chart then will be a guide in the preparation of the ledger, giving account titles and locations. It provides a summary, or bird's-eye view, of the accounts. It also provides a basis for the preparation of a manual of instructions, a book describing how the records are to be kept.

2. *An index to accounts used.* Regardless of the system which has been followed in arranging the accounts in the ledger, it is desirable to have a chart of accounts which serves as an index to the ledger. This not only enables the accounts to be found more readily, but aids in preparation of entries, as it indicates the precise account titles or code designations to be used.

3. *A list of code numbers for ready reference.* When code numbers or symbols are used, they should appear on the chart of accounts with the full names of the accounts, in order to provide a schedule for ready reference and thus facilitate the use of the code designations.

---

4 An example appears in Appendix A, page 189. The chart of accounts is frequently called classification, schedule, table, card, or list of accounts.

4. *An aid in using a uniform accounting system.* In a number of lines of business enterprise, a uniform accounting system for the entire industry has been developed either by a regulatory body or voluntarily by the industry through its trade association. Where such a uniform system is used, a complete chart of accounts is especially valuable as an aid to the intelligent operation of the system and the achievement of uniform results. The chart is useful for the reasons already outlined; it indicates the accounts which are authorized for the system, and it tends to simplify the use of the manual of instructions.

5. *An aid in preparation of reports.* Preparation of financial reports is facilitated by the use of a chart of accounts which indicates the names and locations of the accounts containing the information for such reports. This is of particular value when the accounts are arranged in statement order, as the classes and sub-classes of accounts can then be indicated on the chart of accounts as they will appear on the reports. In some cases the reports themselves indicate the numbers or symbols of the accounts which make up each item contained therein.

THE TRIAL BALANCE

A trial balance is a list of the ledger accounts at a specified date, showing their balances, or the debit and credit totals for each, in debit and credit amount columns. The totals of the two columns should be equal. When this is true, the ledger is said to be in balance.

The trial balance serves the following purposes:

1. It proves the equality of the total debits and credits in the ledger, thus providing at least a partial check on the accuracy of the bookkeeping.

2. It can be an aid in the detection of errors.

3. It furnishes a condensed picture of each account and a summary of all of the accounts.

4. It may be used as a basis for the preparation of the financial statements.

The trial balance is prepared periodically, usually at the end of each month. Either plain, ruled, or columnar paper may be used. The trial balance requires at least three columns: the first for the account titles, the second for the debit amounts, and the third for the credit amounts. Ledger page numbers or account numbers may be listed also.

Methods of Preparation. Two methods of procedure may be followed in showing the amounts opposite the respective account titles on the trial balance, as suggested in the definition above.

1. *Listing the balance of each account.* Many bookkeepers and accountants prefer to list only the balance of each account, placing all debit balances in the first amount column and all credit balances in the second. This requires less work than the other method, because of the smaller number of figures to be listed and added. In this method balances must be computed before the trial balance is taken, but they are used for the preparation of financial statements and therefore must be ascertained sooner or later in any event. Ordinarily an account without a balance is not listed.

2. *Listing both debit and credit totals of each account.* The total of the debits for each account may be entered opposite the account title in the debit column, and the total of the credits in the credit column. This method serves to indicate the total amount, or volume, of the entries in each account instead of the difference between the debits and credits. Such information may

be desirable at times. Accounts which have debits and credits of the same amount may or may not be listed, since the equality of the trial balance totals will not be affected either by the presence or the absence of the same amount in both the debit and credit columns.

It may be desired occasionally to combine the two methods described above by listing only the balances for some accounts and total debits and total credits for others.

Mistakes Not Disclosed by Trial Balance. The trial balance is a valuable accounting tool. It indicates that the debits and credits in the ledger are equal, which is necessary for a correct record, but it does not prove, thereby, that the books are entirely without errors. Mistakes may have occurred which the trial balance does not disclose, as follows:

1. *Compensating errors.* These are mathematical errors of the same amount, often called counter errors, which offset or neutralize each other. They may appear in both debit and credit columns or in one column only. Their presence in the trial balance may result from the fact that errors were made in taking the trial balance, or they may result from errors made in the books of original entry or in the ledger.

2. *Posting to wrong account.* An item may be posted, or entered, in the wrong ledger account although it is indicated properly in the journal, or book of original entry. This type of error will not disturb the equality of debits and credits if the amount appears on the proper side of the ledger even if it is in the wrong account.

3. *Incorrect classification in journal.* An erroneous classification of a transaction in a book of original entry will cause the information to be carried to the wrong account in the ledger.

4. *Transactions not recorded.* If a transaction is not recorded at all, it will have no effect on the debits and

credits. Whether or not it appears in a book of original entry, if a transaction is not recorded in the ledger it will have no effect on the debits and credits of the accounts, and its absence will not be disclosed by the trial balance.

Cause of Unequal Trial Balance Totals. If a trial balance is out of balance, the difference between the totals is caused by one or more mistakes. Such errors may have occurred in the trial balance, the ledger, or the books of original entry. They can be classified as follows:

1. *Errors in addition or subtraction.* Any error in computing totals or balances in the records will disturb the equilibrium of the debits and credits unless it is neutralized by one or more compensating errors.

2. *Listing figures on wrong side of an account.* If a debit is shown on the credit side of an account, or a credit appears as a debit, such errors will cause a discrepancy between the trial balance totals unless offset by other errors.

3. *Listing incorrect figures.* The trial balance may not balance because an amount has been copied incorrectly somewhere in the records. This type of error is likely to occur in one of the following ways:

   a. *Duplicate posting of a debit or credit.* Two entries may be made in error for one debit or credit amount.

   b. *Incorrect copying of one or more digits.* An amount may be incorrect because one or more of its digits is written incorrectly.

   c. *Transposition of figures.* Digits may become transposed when an amount is being copied. An 87 may be written 78, or 162 may appear as 261.

d. *Transplacement of figures.* Any of the digits of a number may be moved one or more spaces to the right or to the left, making a transplacement, or slide, as when 87 is written 870, or 8.70, or 800.70.

4. *Omission of amounts.* An amount may be omitted entirely, causing the records to be out of balance.

ADDITIONAL BIBLIOGRAPHY*

Bolon, Dallas S., *Introduction to Accounting*, 2nd ed. New York: John Wiley & Sons, Inc., 1938. Pp. 28-44, 49-102.

Cole, Dana F., *Beginning Accounting.* New York: Thomas Y. Crowell Co., 1940. Pp. 16-19, 81-128, 150-159, 283-291.

Elwell, Fayette H., *Elementary Accounting.* Boston: Ginn and Co., 1945. Pp. 36-44, 68-71, 79-90, 265-288.

Hatfield, Henry R., Sanders, Thomas H., and Burton, Norman L., *Accounting Principles and Practices.* Boston: Ginn and Co., 1940. Pp. 17-18, 67-101, 112-113.

Howard, Stanley E., *The A B C of Accounting*, 3rd ed. Princeton: Princeton University Press, 1938. Pp. 52-66.

Jackson, J. Hugh, *Accounting Principles.* Los Angeles: Charles R. Hadley Co., 1944. Pp. 11-41, 94-106.

Kelley, Arthur C., *Essentials of Accounting.* New York: American Book Co., 1935. Pp. 28-48, 65-71.

Kennedy, Donald D., Esterly, George R., and von Minden, William J., *Introductory Accounting.* New York: The Ronald Press Co., 1942. Pp. 85-113, 231-250.

Lamberton, Robert A., *Fundamentals of Accounting.* New York: Longmans, Green and Co., 1942. Pp. 41-69.

Prickett, Alva L., and Mikesell, R. Merrill, *Principles of Accounting*, rev. ed. New York: The Macmillan Co., 1937. Pp. 36-64.

Rorem, C. Rufus, *Accounting Method*, 2nd ed. Chicago: The University of Chicago Press, 1930. Pp. 32-89, 411-429.

Scovill, Hiram T., and Moyer, C. A., *Fundamentals of Accounting.* Boston: D. C. Heath and Co., 1940. Pp. 45-68, 108-151, 272-304, 730-733.

* For other references, see the QUICK REFERENCE TABLE TO STANDARD TEXTBOOKS in the forepart of this book.

V

The Journal and Bookkeeping Procedures

PRELIMINARY RECORDS

Ledger an Incomplete Record. A business enterprise needs a ledger to provide a cumulative analysis of the effects of its transactions, but the use of a ledger alone is not satisfactory. Although it is possible to record transactions directly in the ledger accounts, such procedure usually is inadvisable. It fails to meet all of the requirements of a complete accounting system. Various reasons why the ledger is an incomplete record are as follows:

1. *Chronological history not available.* A business enterprise should keep a chronological record of its transactions in order to simplify references to its activities according to date. Ledger accounts do not provide such a record; therefore a day-to-day history of the business is lacking when only a ledger is used.

2. *Information disconnected.* Ordinarily each transaction affects more than one account. When the debits and credits necessary to record a transaction are entered in the accounts, they become separated and the complete transaction is not shown in one place.

3. *Details inadequate.* Only meager information concerning a transaction can be shown conveniently in the account.

4. *Division of labor hampered.* Only one person at a time can efficiently make entries in the ledger. He

43

must have the entire ledger available in order to record the transactions in each account affected. A large enterprise, with a multitude of transactions to record, must use a more efficient system. Its recording process must permit many employees to work on the books at the same time.

5. *Errors difficult to locate.* Making the entries directly in the ledger increases the probability that errors will occur and makes errors more difficult to locate and correct. The following are examples:

   a. Omitting one part of a transaction

   b. Entering part of a transaction on the wrong side of an account

   c. Entering the wrong amount in an account

   d. Entering an amount in the wrong account.

These five reasons make it desirable that an accounting system contain a preliminary record where the transactions will be shown in chronological order, complete in one place, and with adequate explanations as to their nature.

THE DAYBOOK

The daybook is a book of original entry in which a memorandum record of transactions is made in chronological order.[1] It is an informal record, providing the basis for the journal entries. It is rarely used at present, but its functions are performed in many enterprises by a variety of auxiliary records (described in Chapter VIII), including registers and such business papers as sales slips and invoices.

THE JOURNAL

The journal is a chronological record of the transactions of a business. It is a book of original entry in which trans-

---

1 The daybook is also called blotter, jotter, or memorial.

actions are recorded in their chronological order, showing
date for each, amounts and accounts to be debited and
credited, and an explanation. The journal is considered to be
the book of first entry despite the fact that its entries may be
based on memoranda, previously prepared in auxiliary records, which give the details of the transactions. Outstanding
features of the journal may be classified as follows:

1. *A chronological record.* A day-by-day history of the
   transactions of the enterprise is provided.

2. *A debit and credit analysis of transactions.* Each transaction must be analyzed to ascertain its debit and
   credit elements when it is recorded in the journal. The
   journal analysis provides the information needed in
   the ledger.

3. *A brief explanation of each transaction.* All transactions do not need an extensive explanation in the
   books, but there should be enough details in the explanation to help recall the essential features.

Form of General Journal. Any business transaction can
be recorded in a simple journal. An enterprise may use
several journals in which to record special phases of its activities, but it will ordinarily need one additional journal for
miscellaneous entries. This is the *general journal,* sometimes
referred to merely as the *journal.* Its form characteristically
embodies two amount columns at the right, one for debits
and the other for credits. An illustration follows.

Journal

(1)	(2)	(3)	(4)	(5)

The columns provide space for the following information:
(1) date, (2) account title and explanation, (3) ledger folio
—L. F., (4) debit amount, and (5) credit amount. This
has become a standard form for the general journal and is

widely used although variations are employed. Some enterprises find that the efficiency of the general journal is improved by the use of more than two amount columns, the additional columns providing space in which to enter debits and credits that occur frequently enough to make their segregation in special columns desirable. Chapter VII discusses special columns and special journals.

JOURNALIZING

Recording transactions in a journal is known as *journalizing*. Before a transaction can be recorded in a journal, it is necessary to analyze the transaction and decide what accounts should be debited and what accounts should be credited. A broad definition of the term journalizing refers to both (1) the preliminary analysis of the transaction and (2) the actual recording in the journal.

The record of a transaction in a journal is called a *journal entry*. Ordinarily a journal entry relates to one transaction, but it may be used to record a group of transactions. A complete journal entry contains equal debit and credit amounts, following the fundamental rule of accounting—for every debit there must be a credit.

Content of the Journal Entry. Each entry in the two-column journal normally contains the following six parts:

1. *Date.* The date of the transaction to be recorded may be placed in the date column at the left side of the journal page on the line used for the first debit item. The year should be shown at the top of the page. Where two date columns are used, the name of the month is placed in one and the day of the month in the other. Frequently the name of the month is omitted from all but the first entry on a page. The date may be placed at the middle of the journal page on the line immediately above each entry, showing either the month, day, and year, or the day only, with the month and year written at the top of the page. It is

customary to leave one or two blank lines between entries in the general journal, but no blank lines within an entry, so that the record of each transaction is clearly distinguishable.

2. *Titles of accounts to be debited.* The title of each account to be debited is written on a separate line in the column used for account titles and explanation, starting at the left edge of that column. The accounts named in a journal entry indicate the ledger accounts affected by the entry. Care should be exercised that the exact account titles used in the ledger appear in the journal. This helps to find the right account in the ledger quickly and avoids confusion where names of accounts are somewhat similar. Debits usually precede credits in a general journal entry.

3. *Debit amounts.* Any debit amounts relating to the transaction are entered in the left-hand amount column opposite their respective account titles.

4. *Titles of accounts to be credited.* The title of each account to be credited is written in the account and explanation column, uniformly indented from the left edge, and beginning on the line immediately following the last debit item.

5. *Credit amounts.* Any credit amounts relating to the transaction are entered in the right-hand amount column opposite their respective account titles.

6. *Explanation.* It is desirable to include an explanation with each entry in the general journal. The description may be brief, but it should be sufficient to help recall full particulars if reference is made to the transaction later. There is no one standard form, but many bookkeepers start the explanation on the line

immediately following the last credit item, writing only in the account and explanation column.

Simple and Compound Journal Entries. An entry in a journal which contains only one debit item and one credit item is called a simple journal entry. If more than one debit and one credit are necessary, the entry is a compound journal entry. Following is an example of a simple journal entry, made on September 1, and a compound journal entry, made on September 2:

Journal

1940			
Sept. 1	Cash	15,000.00	
	J. Jones, Proprietorship		15,000.00
	Invested cash for the purpose of establishing the Jones H a r d w a r e Store		
2	Land	2,000.00	
	Building	7,000.00	
	Furniture and Fixtures	1,000.00	
	Cash		10,000.00
	To record purchase of land, building, and fixtures for cash		

POSTING

The transfer of debit and credit items listed in a journal to their respective accounts in a ledger is called *posting*.

Each debit item in an ordinary two-column journal is posted to the ledger by entering in the debit column of the proper account the amount shown in the debit column of the journal opposite that account title. Each credit item is posted by entering in the credit column of the proper account the amount shown in the credit column of the journal opposite that account title. In the process of posting, the debit and credit items may be taken in any order desired. For instance, all debits may be posted before the credits. Many bookkeepers see no decided advantage in this, however, and prefer to post the items in the order in which they appear in the journal.

As each item is posted, the number of the ledger account (or the page number) to which it is posted is entered in the folio column of the journal on the line on which the item appears. At the same time, the page number of the journal is placed in the folio column of the ledger account on the line on which the item is posted. This is sometimes called *paging*. The folio columns thus provide a cross reference to simplify the tracing of entries. The journal folio column also performs an important service in showing whether or not an item has been posted. Check marks sometimes are used instead of numbers, especially if neither the accounts nor the ledger pages are numbered. Either check marks or numbers should be placed in the journal folio column at the time of posting, so that blank spaces in the column will indicate items that are still to be posted.[2]

RELATION BETWEEN JOURNAL AND LEDGER

The journal and the ledger are the basic books of a double-entry accounting system. Both books are essential to a complete and efficient accounting system. The journal is the chronological record, and the ledger is the analytical record. The journal is the book of original entry; the ledger is the book of second entry, a derived record. The journal, as a book of first entry, ordinarily has greater weight as legal evidence than the ledger.

---

2 Some bookkeepers enter the account numbers with the account titles when making a journal entry, and place a check mark beside each amount in the journal when it is posted.

ADDITIONAL BIBLIOGRAPHY*

Bolon, Dallas S., *Introduction to Accounting*, 2nd ed. New York: John Wiley & Sons, Inc., 1938. Pp. 44-50.

Cole, Dana F., *Beginning Accounting*. New York: Thomas Y. Crowell Co., 1940. Pp. 26-27, 140-150.

Elwell, Fayette H., *Elementary Accounting*. Boston: Ginn and Co., 1945. Pp. 45-55, 71-79.

Hatfield, Henry R., Sanders, Thomas H., and Burton, Norman L., *Accounting Principles and Practices*. Boston: Ginn and Co., 1940. Pp. 102-111.

Howard, Stanley E., *The A B C of Accounting*, 3rd ed. Princeton: Princeton University Press, 1938. Pp. 52, 67-72.

Jackson, J. Hugh, *Accounting Principles*. Los Angeles: Charles R. Hadley Co., 1944. Pp. 26-35.

Kelley, Arthur C., *Essentials of Accounting*. New York: American Book Co., 1935. Pp. 62-65.

Kennedy, Donald D., Esterly, George R., and von Minden, William J., *Introductory Accounting*. New York: The Ronald Press Co., 1942. Pp. 251-254.

Lamberton, Robert A., *Fundamentals of Accounting*. New York: Longmans, Green and Co., 1942. Pp. 70-91.

Prickett, Alva L., and Mikesell, R. Merrill, *Principles of Accounting*, rev. ed. New York: The Macmillan Co., 1937. Pp. 65-92.

Rorem, C. Rufus, *Accounting Method*, 2nd ed. Chicago: The University of Chicago Press, 1930. Pp. 61-73.

Scovill, Hiram T., and Moyer, C. A., *Fundamentals of Accounting*. Boston: D. C. Heath and Co., 1940. Pp. 152-166.

---

* For other references, see the QUICK REFERENCE TABLE TO STANDARD TEXTBOOKS in the forepart of this book.

Periodic Adjustments and Summarization

CASH AND ACCRUAL BASES OF ACCOUNTING

Cash Basis. If the cash basis is used in keeping the books, income is recorded only when cash is received and expense is recognized only when cash is paid out.

The cash basis is often modified to include the recording of accounts payable, accounts receivable, and depreciation. If depreciation is recognized, it is computed periodically in the same manner as if the business were on the accrual basis. An enterprise which has a merchandise inventory cannot ordinarily operate effectively on the cash basis.

The cash method of accounting is frequently used by professional men, non-profit organizations, and small businesses, and by individuals for personal and family records.

Accrual Basis. The accrual basis offers a more accurate method of accounting than the cash basis. When the accrual basis is used, income is recorded for the fiscal period in which it is earned, whether it is received during that period or not. Expenses incurred in earning the income are recorded as expense, whether or not payment has been made for them during that period. The resulting profit and loss statement includes only such incomes as were earned during the period covered by the statement and such expenses as relate to the same period.

A problem which sometimes presents difficulties involves determination of the date on which income may be said to be earned, and proper allocation of expenses to that income. Solution of such a problem generally requires consideration of all the known factors. When the accrual basis is employed, the financial statements usually cannot be prepared from the trial balance of the ledger accounts as they appear when only the entries for the ordinary operations of the business have been posted. Complete and accurate balance sheets and profit and loss statements depend upon the inclusion of various income and expense items that have accrued from day to day and have not been recorded currently in the accounts. It is not practical or convenient to record this information daily; in fact, some necessary information is not readily available except at longer intervals. It is not necessary to make daily changes, since the complete information is needed only at the end of the accounting period.

THE ACCOUNTING PERIOD

The time covered by the statement of profit and loss or the time which has elapsed between two succeeding balance sheets is the *accounting period*. It is also called the *fiscal period*. Enterprises ordinarily have an accounting period one year in length, which may or may not coincide with the calendar year. However, this may be broken down into other accounting periods, so that in addition to the annual financial statements, the enterprise will prepare more frequent reports, especially semi-annual, quarterly, and monthly reports.

TYPES OF ACCRUED AND
DEFERRED ITEMS

Use of the accrual method of accounting gives rise to a number of accrued and deferred items. The existence of these items is due to the fact that many of the income and expense transactions relate to more than one period.

Some of these items are discussed later in this chapter, but the groups into which they are classified are as follows:

1. *Accrued income* is income earned for which payment is not due to be received until a subsequent period or periods.

2. *Accrued expense* is an expense of the present period for which payment is due to be made in a subsequent period.

3. *Deferred income* is income received but not yet earned.

4. *Deferred expense* represents commodities or services purchased for use in the business but not consumed at the end of the accounting period.

ADJUSTMENTS

Adjusting Entries. An adjusting entry may be made at any time that an account needs adjustment. The term adjusting entries, however, refers particularly to the periodic entries made at the close of an accounting period to bring the ledger accounts up to date. Mixed accounts are adjusted in order to separate the real from the nominal elements. It will be found that every adjusting entry involves at least one real account and at least one nominal account.

Common Types of Adjustments. There are four common types of adjustments. These adjustments are discussed in detail later in this chapter. The four types may be classified as follows:

1. *Merchandise inventory*

2. *Accrued and deferred items*

3. *Depreciation*

4. *Bad debts.*

Correcting Entries. A distinction sometimes is made between adjusting entries, discussed above, and correcting entries. When errors are discovered in the accounts, they may be rectified through the use of correcting entries. Such entries ordinarily should be made when the errors are found. This may be during the accounting period, at the close of the period, or during a subsequent period.

THE WORK SHEET

The work sheet, or working sheet, is a columnar device which enables the unadjusted account balances shown in the trial balance to be adjusted and segregated into balance sheet and profit and loss statement items. The work sheet is an accountant's device used to facilitate preparation of the periodic financial statements. The accountant, therefore, uses any one of the various forms available which is best suited to his needs.

One form of 10-column work sheet is as follows:

Name of Account	Trial Balance		Adjustments		Adjusted Trial Balance		Profit & Loss Statement		Balance Sheet	
	Dr.	Cr.	Dr.	Cr.	Dr.	Cr.	Dr.	Cr.	Dr.	Cr.

Steps in Preparation of a 10-Column Work Sheet. The following are steps in the preparation of one type of the 10-column work sheet.

1. In the trial balance columns, enter the balances of the ledger accounts as they appear before the adjusting and closing entries are made. Add the debit and credit columns, which must have equal totals.

2. In the adjustments columns, enter all adjusting entries.

3. In the adjusted trial balance columns, extend the trial balance, giving effect to the adjustments.

4. Distribute the income and expense accounts to the profit and loss statement columns and the asset, liability, and proprietorship accounts to the balance sheet columns.

Variations in the Work Sheet Columns. Work sheets may have more or fewer columns than the 10-column work sheet illustrated above.

1. The *8-column* work sheet omits the adjusted trial balance columns. It is frequently used by accountants, as it distributes the adjusted account balances directly to the profit and loss statement and balance sheet columns without the extra work of entering them first in the adjusted trial balance columns.

2. The *6-column* work sheet omits the adjustments columns, but it is used infrequently.

3. The *12-column* work sheet for a mercantile concern may include a pair of columns for additional information, such as the trading account, cost of sales, cost of goods sold, or surplus.

4. *Multi-column* work sheets, including 10, 12, or more columns, are frequently used by manufacturing concerns and occasionally by mercantile concerns.

Effects Achieved by the Work Sheet are indicated by this list of its purposes, uses, and advantages.

1. The usual form of trial balance is provided to determine whether the debits and credits in the ledger are equal.

2. A summary of the accounts is provided which shows the results of the fiscal period and gives the accountant a panoramic, bird's-eye view of the enterprise.

3. Reference to previous work sheets enables the accountant to plan the work for the close of the accounting period and facilitates adjustment and closing of the books.

4. Adjustments of accounts for inventories, **accruals**, etc., are made tentatively, and their accuracy is proved before they are actually entered upon the journal and ledger.

5. The mathematical accuracy of entries, accounts, and statements is known before the books are closed.

6. The profit or loss for the accounting period may be known quickly, in fact, even before the books are adjusted and closed or the statements are prepared.

7. The work sheet usually supplies the information necessary for the preparation of the formal adjusting and closing entries.

8. Classification and segregation of assets, liabilities, incomes, and expenses are provided.

9. Preparation of financial statements is facilitated by the work sheet. In fact, the statements may be prepared from the work sheet without the necessity of previously entering the adjusting and closing entries in the book.

10. Interim statements may be prepared at monthly or other intervals without formally closing the books.

CLOSING ENTRIES

Closing entries are periodic entries made at the end of accounting periods to close the temporary proprietorship accounts, consisting of the income, expense, and summarizing accounts. These entries arise from the necessity of segregating and summarizing the incomes and expenses for each fiscal period to determine the net gain or loss for the period.

The profit and loss statement may be used as a guide in preparation of the closing entries, or these entries may be prepared from the profit and loss columns of the work sheet, as mentioned above.

A two-fold purpose is accomplished by the closing entries, as follows:

1. Clear the nominal accounts of the transactions of the past fiscal period.

2. Show in the proper proprietorship accounts the net effects of all operations of the fiscal period.

Closing entries are entries used to transfer the balances of the nominal, or temporary proprietorship, accounts to proprietorship. This is usually done by means of an intermediate summarization account, or clearing account, Profit and Loss.

The closing entries may be separated into two distinct steps. The first step is to close all open income and expense accounts to the Profit and Loss account. The second step is to close the Profit and Loss account to proprietorship.

BALANCING AND RULING
THE ACCOUNTS

The asset, liability, and proprietorship accounts which have a balance at the close of the fiscal period are balanced by writing the word *Balance* in the description column of the smaller side, blank checking the folio column, and entering in the money column the amount of difference between the pencil footings previously computed. Then the total of both debits and credits is taken and written on the same line in the account. A double ruling is placed below the totals and across all columns except the explanation or description columns. Below the double ruling, on what was the larger side, the date is entered, the word *Balance* is written in the description column, the folio column is blank checked, and the amount of the difference, or balance, is written in the money column.

All accounts which do not have a balance remaining at the end of the fiscal period are totaled and double ruled underneath the totals. If there is only one entry on each side of an account and they are for equal amounts, the double ruling is usually considered to be sufficient.

POST-CLOSING TRIAL BALANCE

A trial balance may be taken of the ledger after all adjusting and closing entries have been journalized and posted and the accounts have been balanced and ruled. Such a trial balance is termed the *post-closing trial balance*. This is done for the purpose of verifying the correctness of such work. The post-closing trial balance, as ordinarily prepared, may be checked against the formal balance sheet for additional verification.

REVERSING ENTRIES

After the ledger has been closed, the balances of the accounts representing accrued and deferred items, which consist of accrued expenses, deferred charges to expense, accrued income, and deferred credits to income, remain on the books as assets and liabilities. A customary procedure is to transfer them to the respective income and expense accounts to which they relate and from which they came. The transferring entries, ordinarily termed reversing, reversal, readjusting, or post-closing entries, are made in the general journal. They are usually entered before the ordinary business transactions of the new fiscal period, but they may be delayed until the close of the fiscal period.

An alternative procedure, which avoids the use of reversing entries, is to close the accrued and deferred accounts when transactions occur to which they relate. Reversing entries are sometimes discussed along with the closing entries, since they are a part of the periodic adjustment and summarization process.

THE ACCOUNTING CYCLE

The accounting cycle, or bookkeeping cycle, as worked out up to this time, contains the following steps:

1. Journalize ordinary business transactions
2. Post and prove journal
3. Foot the accounts and take the trial balance
4. Determine the adjustments, such as inventories, accruals, etc.
5. Complete the work sheet
6. Prepare financial statements and schedules
7. Journalize and post adjusting entries
8. Journalize and post the closing entries
9. Balance and rule the accounts
10. Take post-closing trial balance.

MERCHANDISE INVENTORY

In a mercantile enterprise the merchandise consists of goods acquired for resale. An inventory, or count, of such merchandise is ordinarily taken at regular intervals, at least at the close of each fiscal year.

Merchandise Inventory is an asset account recording in monetary terms the merchandise held for resale. Procedures ordinarily used in accounting for merchandise may be classified into two groups, the physical inventory and the perpetual inventory. Variations in these procedures are frequent.

Physical Inventory. The physical, or periodic, inventory method is commonly used. In this method an actual count is made of the merchandise on hand at the end of each accounting period. The amount so determined is carried in the Merchandise Inventory account unchanged until the close of the succeeding period, when the account is adjusted to show the amount of the new inventory.

There are various ways to adjust the Merchandise Inventory account, of which the following three ways are representative.

1. *Adjustment through Profit and Loss account.* The Profit and Loss account is used as a summarization account in adjusting Merchandise Inventory. The old inventory is closed out by such an entry as this:

> Profit and Loss
>
> Merchandise Inventory

The amount of the new inventory is then recorded by this entry:

> Merchandise Inventory
>
> Profit and Loss

The Merchandise Inventory and Profit and Loss accounts will appear like this:

Merchandise Inventory

Inventory (old)	Inventory (old) to Profit and Loss
Inventory (new)	

Profit and Loss

Inventory (old)	Inventory (new)

The Purchases account and other accounts relating to merchandise will be closed to the Profit and Loss account.

This method of adjusting the Merchandise Inventory account is frequently used, especially in small businesses. Its use is particularly advantageous in that, first, the same form may be used regardless of the comparative sizes of the old inventory, the new inventory, and purchases; and second, all the detailed information needed for the preparation of the profit and loss statement is available in one place, the Profit and Loss account. Some authorities prefer to accomplish the same results by making these entries closing rather than adjusting entries.

2. *Adjustment through Cost of Goods Sold account.* The Cost of Goods Sold account is another summarization account used by accountants in the adjustment of the Merchandise Inventory account. When the Cost of Goods Sold account is used, several variations in entries may be employed, but one typical way will illustrate its use. The old inventory figure is closed by such an entry as:

> Cost of Goods Sold
>
> > Merchandise Inventory

The new inventory figure may be recorded by this entry:

> Merchandise Inventory
>
> > Cost of Goods Sold

The balance of Purchases and related accounts will be transferred to the Cost of Goods Sold account by such entries as:

> Cost of Goods Sold
>
> > Purchases
> >
> > Freight In

and:

> Purchase Returns
>
> Purchase Allowances
>
> Cost of Goods Sold

The Cost of Goods Sold account will be closed to the Profit and Loss account by one of the closing entries.

While this method of adjusting Merchandise Inventory does not give the detailed information used in preparation of the profit and loss statement in one place, it does provide a summary of the cost of goods sold which otherwise is available only in the profit and loss statement.

3. *Adjustment through Purchases account.* Purchases account may be used as a summarization account in a third method of adjusting the Merchandise Inventory account. In such instances, the Purchases account is used similarly to the Cost of Goods Sold account. The old inventory is closed to it, the new inventory is set up out of it, and the various related accounts are closed into it. The balance of the Purchases account is then cost of goods sold and will be closed into the Profit and Loss account by one of the closing entries.

This is only one of many ways in which the Purchases account may be utilized in adjusting the Merchandise Inventory account.

Perpetual Inventory. The perpetual inventory method requires the keeping of a continuous record of all goods on hand. In order that this may be done, an additional entry is required at the time each sale is made. A cash purchase is recorded as follows:

> Merchandise
>
> **Cash**

At the time a cash sale is made the usual entry is:

>   Cash
>   Sales

This is accompanied by the following entry, the amounts being the cost price of the goods sold:

>   Cost of Goods Sold
>   Merchandise

When these entries have been posted to the accounts, the accounts affecting merchandise appear as follows:

Merchandise	
Purchases	Cost price of goods sold

Sales	
	Sale price of goods sold

Cost of Goods Sold	
Merchandise (cost of goods sold)	

The Merchandise account having been debited for the purchases and credited for the cost price of the goods sold, the balance purports to be the cost of the merchandise on hand. Since this does not take into consideration merchandise which may have been broken or stolen by either employees or customers, a periodic, or physical, inventory should be taken and the Merchandise account adjusted. Variations in the method of recording the perpetual inventory are found and additional techniques may be employed.

The perpetual inventory is not satisfactory for some merchandising concerns since the physical inventory must still be made and since the cost of goods sold is sometimes difficult to compute for each transaction. However, the perpetual inventory is frequently used by manufacturing enterprises.

Other Inventory Procedures. Two additional variations in the method of handling Merchandise Inventory may be noted.

1. *A single mixed merchandise account is sometimes used.* In this account all information relating to merchandise may be placed, including inventories, purchases, sales, and the various adjunct accounts. It is a mixed account, since it contains incomes, expenses, and assets. A mixed merchandise account is used by some teachers as an introduction to the teaching of the handling of merchandise. Such an account is seldom used in business since an analysis and summarization must be made of the entries in the account to provide the detailed information necessary for the preparation of the profit and loss statement, and for the use of the executives in charge of merchandise activities.

2. *The estimated inventory method is sometimes used to compute gross profit.* In enterprises in which the ratio of gross profit to sales is accurately computed and relatively steady, an estimate of gross profits based on this ratio will make possible an estimation of the amount of the merchandise inventory. The estimated inventory method may be used for enterprises which desire that financial statements be prepared more frequently than the physical inventories are made. The use of this method is not ordinarily intended to supplant one of the other methods, but only to supplement its usefulness.

The adjustment of the Merchandise Inventory account is a necessary step in the allocating of costs. Allocation of costs must be extended to supplies and other costs which may be only partially consumed in a single accounting period, in order that a more accurate expense figure may be computed. This is true in a mercantile enterprise, and is even more evident in accounting for the goods in the process of manufacturing in a manufacturing enterprise.

In a manufacturing enterprise the one account for merchandise inventory is replaced with three separate inventories, Raw Materials Inventory, Goods in Process Inventory, and Finished Goods Inventory. These accounts will be discussed in greater detail in a subsequent chapter.

ACCRUED AND DEFERRED ITEMS

Interest and Discount. *Interest* is compensation for the use of money. Interest is usually paid at the maturity of a short-term note, or is paid quarterly, semi-annually, or annually on a long-term note or bond. When interest is collected in advance it is termed *discount.* Borrowing money from banks usually consists in discounting a note, which means that the bank collects the interest for the life of the note at the time the obligation is made. All notes may be said to earn interest, even though they state that they are non-interest-bearing obligations. The present value of any note is its maturity value less its discount to the present time. If a non-interest-bearing note is received from a customer, the interest which is foregone may be said to be an additional sales discount given the customer.

On notes receivable a proportionate share of the interest is earned each day. When using the accrual method, it is necessary at the close of each fiscal period to adjust the interest account to take into consideration any unpaid interest which an obligation has earned during that fiscal period. That interest which has been earned but not yet received is termed *accrued interest receivable,* while interest that has been received but not yet earned is termed *interest received in advance.* The interest expense arising from notes payable must also be adjusted at the end of each fiscal period. Interest which has been paid but not yet consumed is termed *prepaid interest,* while interest which has been consumed but not yet paid is termed *accrued interest payable.*

Insurance. Insurance premiums, under ordinary circumstances, are paid before the insurance goes into effect, at which time the amount paid is considered prepaid insurance. As each day passes, a proportionate share of that premium is consumed and becomes insurance expense. In this instance, however, as in the case of most accrued and deferred items, the amount of the expense is not computed day by day, but adjustment is made only at the close of the fiscal period. At that time the asset account is decreased, and the expense account is established for the amount of the expired insurance.

An alternate method of handling insurance premiums is sometimes used. In this method the full amount of the premium paid is debited to Insurance Expense at the time of payment. At the close of the fiscal period Prepaid Insurance is debited and Insurance Expense is credited for the amount of the unexpired insurance. The first method considers it an expense when acquired. Both methods achieve the same results when the accounts are adjusted at the close of the fiscal period.

Supplies. At the time of the acquisition, supplies may be considered either as an asset or as an expense. If supplies are treated as an asset when acquired, it is necessary at the close of the fiscal period, when an inventory of supplies is taken, to decrease the asset account for the amount of supplies consumed and set up a Supplies Used account or a Supplies Expense account. If supplies are considered as an expense when acquired, an asset account will be set up at the end of the fiscal period for the amount of supplies found to be on hand by the supplies inventory, and the expense account will be decreased by the amount.

Various Other Accounts are adjusted at the close of each fiscal period in a manner similar to that indicated above. Some examples are: rent, commissions, wages, and royalties. These may be either income or expense accounts.

Effects on the Accounts. Accrued and deferred items, such as those discussed in the preceding part of this chapter, have the following effects on the accounts when the adjustments are recorded:

Adjustment	Dr.	Cr.
Income earned but not previously recorded	Asset (increase)	Income (increase)
Expense accrued but not yet paid and not previously recorded	Expense (increase)	Liability (increase)
Income received in advance and credited to income when received or	Income (decrease)	Liability (increase)
income received in advance and credited to a liability account when received	Liability (decrease)	Income (increase)
Expense paid in advance and debited to expense when paid or	Asset (increase)	Expense (decrease)
expense paid in advance and debited to an asset account when paid	Expense (increase)	Asset (decrease)

DEPRECIATION AND DEPLETION

Depreciation may be defined as the decrease in the value of a fixed asset which is due to the effect of the passage of time, wear and tear, obsolescence, and inadequacy. Depreciation is both physical and non-physical. The physical factor includes deterioration due to the passage of time and the action of the elements, and also the wear and tear due to the use of the asset. The non-physical factor includes supersession, or inadequacy, which is due to the need for replacing an asset with a larger unit, and obsolescence, which is due to inventions or other changes in assets which make it desirable to replace present units with more efficient ones.

The recording of depreciation is done to meet a two-fold purpose: first, to value the asset, and second, to distribute the cost of the asset over its useful life.

Methods of Computing Depreciation. The most commonly used method of computing depreciation is the straight line method. In this method the life of the asset is estimated and an equal part of the depreciable value of the asset is charged off for each accounting period during the life of the asset. The depreciable value is computed by subtracting the estimated scrap value from the original cost.

The straight line method is used because it is the easiest to compute and to use, and also because in many instances no other method can be shown to be definitely more accurate.

Because of the great variety of assets which are used by business enterprises, there must of necessity be a variety of ways of computing the depreciation on such assets so that the depreciation will be as nearly as possible in accord with the facts of each case. Methods of computing depreciation fall principally into two classifications: methods which consider depreciation a function of time and methods which consider depreciation a function of use.

When depreciation is considered as a function of time, it may be computed on the following bases:

1. *An increasing rate, which includes the sinking fund method and the increasing fraction method.* These methods, in their ordinary use, give an increasing charge for depreciation, and the depreciated value tends to measure usefulness.

2. *The straight line method, described above.*

3. *A decreasing rate, which includes the reducing fraction method and uniform rate on a diminishing value method.* Both of these methods give a declining charge for depreciation. The depreciated value, computed by these methods, tends to follow market value.

When depreciation is considered as a function of use, it may be computed on the following bases:

1. The units of production

2. The hours of operation

3. A percentage of sales.

These methods may be further described as follows:

The *sinking fund method* provides that equal amounts shall be paid into a fund each accounting period. The assets in the fund earn a stated rate of interest which is added to the fund so thāt at the end of the useful life of the asset the total in the fund will equal the depreciable value.

The *increasing fraction method*, or *sum of the years method*, computes the charge to depreciation as a fractional part of the depreciable value. The life of the asset is estimated in terms of the number of years of useful life. The denominators of all the fractions are the same, the sum of the numbers of years. The numerators of the fractions are the numbers of the years used in sequence beginning with 1 and increasing each year in consecutive order.

The *reducing fraction method* is computed similarly to the increasing fraction method, discussed above. The difference is that the numerators are the numbers of the fiscal periods used in reverse order.

The *uniform rate on a diminishing value method* is computed by charging a constant percentage against the depreciated balance each year. The 1954 Internal Revenue Code permits this percentage to be twice the percentage that would be allowed with the straight line method.

The *units of production method* charges depreciation in

accordance with the number of units the particular asset has produced during the fiscal period. The life of the asset is estimated in terms of units of production, and the depreciable value is divided by this number of units to determine how much should be charged to depreciation for each unit of production.

The *hours of operation method* charges depreciation in accordance with the number of hours the particular asset has been used during the fiscal period. The life of the asset is estimated in terms of hours of use, and the depreciable value is divided by this number of hours to determine how much should be charged to depreciation for each hour of use.

The *percentage of sales* method computes depreciation as a fixed percentage of the sales. The charge for depreciation varies in direct relation to the volume of production.

Most of the methods of computing depreciation will be found in these classifications and sub-classifications, although special methods are sometimes found relating to special conditions and assets. Some methods not listed in the sub-classifications above, are the following: the annuity method; the discount method; the appraisal, or revaluation, method; the replacement, or renewal, method; and the insurance, or actuarial, method. Various other titles are sometimes given to the methods listed.

Depreciation Rates. Rates of depreciation may be established by an enterprise on the basis of its past experience, or with the assistance of published depreciation tables. Such tables may be found in *Bulletin F* of the United States Bureau of Internal Revenue, in trade association manuals, and in other business publications.

It is desirable to compute depreciation on each individual asset at an appropriate rate determined by its estimated useful life. This may be done under any of the methods listed above. However, a *composite* rate or *blanket* rate may be adopted. Use of the composite rate requires less detailed record keeping, since depreciation is computed for a group of assets at a rate considered to be average for the group.

Methods of Recording Depreciation. The amount of the estimated depreciation relating to a given fiscal period is charged to a depreciation expense account and credited to the proper valuation account as reserve, or allowance, for depreciation of that particular asset. Occasionally a different entry is made. This is a debit to a depreciation expense account and a credit to the asset account involved. This second method obscures the original cost of the asset.

Depletion. The loss of value which accompanies extractive operations on such wasting assets as oil wells, mineral deposits, and timber land, is known as depletion. It is similar to depreciation, but the terms should be distinguished from each other.

Several methods of computing depletion may be followed. One of the commonest is the production method. By such a method the value of the land after the natural resources are removed, is subtracted from the total cost of the asset to give the total depletion. The number of units of the asset to be removed is estimated and this number is divided into the total depletion to give the unit depletion cost. The depletion for the fiscal period is then computed by multiplying the number of units removed during the period by the unit depletion cost.

The depletion may be recorded by debiting an account for depletion expense and crediting a reserve for depletion account.

BAD DEBTS

Bad debts generally are encountered in an enterprise which does business on a credit basis. An uncollectible account is usually found to be uncollectible in an accounting period subsequent to the one in which the sale was made. Sales vary in volume from one accounting period to another, and it is considered desirable to have each period bear the expense for the estimated amount of uncollectible accounts resulting from sales made during the period. In order that each fiscal period may bear the expense that arises from the non-payment of accounts receivable which relate to it, the accounts are adjusted at the end of the period for the estimated loss from bad debts.

Methods of Computing Bad Debts. On the basis of past experience, there are two principal methods of computing the estimated loss from bad debts. One emphasizes the bad debts expense, computing it as a fixed percentage of accounts receivable, total receivables, net sales, or sales on credit. The other emphasizes the reserve for bad debts, adding to the reserve only enough to make the total a predetermined percentage of the accounts receivable, or of the total receivables, at the close of the fiscal period. Under the second method, the amount of bad debts expense is given secondary consideration, being dependent upon the size of the reserve for bad debts.

Various other methods may be used. One is to examine and study the accounts receivable and thus determine what ones are likely to be uncollectible. Such a study may be expedited by *aging* the accounts receivable. Accounts are aged by classifying the unpaid amounts according to date of charge, or according to date due. Another method is to make no adjustments, but merely to charge off individual accounts to bad debts expense when they are determined to be bad. A firm should consider the possible uncollectibility of its notes receivable, loans to employees, and accounts receivable when providing for bad debts.

Methods of Recording Bad Debts. The estimated loss from bad debts for the fiscal period may be charged to Loss from Bad Debts account, or to Bad Debts Expense account, at the close of the fiscal period, and credited to the Reserve, or Allowance, for Bad Debts account, or to the Reserve, or Allowance, for Doubtful accounts.

A loss from an uncollectible account is properly chargeable to the period in which the sale was made. Therefore, adjustment should be made at the close of each fiscal period for the estimated bad debts expense which relates to that fiscal period.

VALUATION ACCOUNTS

Two accounts may be used to show the present estimated net value of a single item. When this is done, one account is used to show the original value, which usually is cost, and the other account to show the estimated decrease in value. The latter account has the smaller balance, is properly subtracted from the historical cost or other basis on the statements, and is called a valuation, offset, or contra account.

Valuation reserves are these accounts which show deductions from asset accounts. For example, the Reserve for Depreciation account contains the accumulated estimated net decrease in the value of the particular asset account to which it pertains. Furthermore, the Reserve for Bad Debts account contains the estimated amount of the accounts receivable which will not be collectible. Other such accounts are Reserve for Depletion and Reserve for Exhaustion. The word *Allowance* is sometimes used in the title of such valuation accounts by writers who consider this word more precise than the more commonly used word *Reserve*.

Each valuation reserve account is shown on the balance sheet directly below the asset to which it pertains. The amount of the valuation reserve is subtracted from the historical cost of the asset, the difference being the present estimated net value of the asset. A valuation reserve account is a negative asset (or minus asset) account.

Some other valuation accounts which are not ordinarily adjusted are the following: Sales Returns and Allowances, Purchase Returns and Allowances, and Discount on Capital Stock.

ADDITIONAL BIBLIOGRAPHY*

Accountants' Handbook, 3rd ed. New York: The Ronald Press Co., 1957. Pp. 11:24-30, 12:1-63, 17:1-56, 22:12-23.

Bolon, Dallas S., *Introduction to Accounting*, 2nd ed. New York: John Wiley & Sons, Inc., 1938, Pp. 72-78, 103-120, 176-276, 422-451.

Cole, Dana F., *Beginning Accounting*. New York: Thomas Y. Crowell Co., 1940. Pp. 65-68, 128-228, 312-383, 668-746.

Elwell, Fayette H., *Elementary Accounting*. Boston: Ginn and Co., 1945. Pp. 111-127, 185-249, 499-534.

Hatfield, Henry R., Sanders, Thomas H., and Burton, Norman L., *Accounting Principles and Practices*. Boston: Ginn and Co., 1940. Pp. 112-156, 304-320.

Howard, Stanley E., *The A B C of Accounting*, 3rd ed. Princeton: Princeton University Press, 1938. Pp. 72-106, 124-153, 157-165, 198-220.

Jackson, J. Hugh, *Accounting Principles*. Los Angeles: Charles R. Hadley Co., 1944. Pp. 45-68, 247-333, 355-370.

Kelley, Arthur C., *Essentials of Accounting*. New York: American Book Co., 1935. Pp. 49-61, 71-85, 103-128, 180-195, 387-390.

Kennedy, Donald D., Esterly, George R., and von Minden, William J., *Introductory Accounting*. New York: The Ronald Press Co., 1942. Pp. 353-444.

Lamberton, Robert A., *Fundamentals of Accounting*. New York: Longmans, Green and Co., 1942. Pp. 152-228.

Mason, Perry, *Principles of Public Utility Depreciation*. Chicago: American Accounting Association, 1937, Chapter 1.

Prickett, Alva L., and Mikesell, R. Merrill, *Principles of Accounting*, rev. ed. New York: The Macmillan Co., 1937, Pp. 107-183.

Rorem, C. Rufus, *Accounting Method*, 2nd ed., Chicago: The University of Chicago Press, 1930. Pp. 110-147, 281-335.

Scovill, Hiram T., and Moyer, C. A., *Fundamentals of Accounting*. Boston: D. C. Heath and Co., 1940. Pp. 68-147, 260-271, 333-386, 517-519.

---

* For other references, see the QUICK REFERENCE TABLE TO STANDARD TEXTBOOKS in the forepart of this book.

Division of the Basic Books

NEED FOR SUBDIVISION

All the transactions of a business may be recorded in a simple two-column journal and a ledger containing the ordinary standard form of accounts. However, such a simple plan for the financial records is not efficient if a large volume of business is transacted. Many business enterprises find that they can use subdivisions of these basic books advantageously. They may classify their transactions and place those types which occur most frequently in special columns in the general journal, or in separate special journals; and when they have a substantial number of accounts they may segregate some of them in subsidiary ledgers.

Special journals and special or subsidiary ledgers are used in enterprises of every size and are considered indispensable for large and complex business organizations.

SPECIAL COLUMNS

Columnar General Journal. Any journal with more than one debit column or more than one credit column is a special-column journal.[1] The introduction of special columns into the general journal provides a simple method for saving time and space in the bookkeeping process. A small enterprise may operate without the help of special journals, but when entries affecting one account occur repeatedly, the

---

1 Special-column journals bear a variety of other descriptive names, such as columnar journals, divided-column journals, multiple-column journals, and multi-column journals.

work of posting can be reduced materially by placing one or more special columns in the general journal.

A special column relates to one general ledger account only, and contains debits only or credits only. It provides an initial segregation of one type of item. Later, usually at the end of the month, the total of the column is posted as one amount. Thus one posting to the ledger account takes the place of a number of entries which would have to be made if each amount appearing in the column were posted separately.

Structure of the Columnar General Journal. The number of special columns to be used is a matter of expediency, varying according to the convenience of those who use them. Too many columns will make the journal unwieldy, a condition which may be prevented by the introduction of special journals. Every additional column also increases the number of spaces in which an amount may be placed erroneously.

Special columns often are used for such accounts as Cash, Accounts Receivable, Accounts Payable, Sales, and Purchases. If separate special journals are desired for some of the transactions, such as cash receipts and disbursements, the general journal may still contain special columns for other common transactions. Whether or not the general journal contains special columns, it does not give up the two columns for *miscellaneous* debits and credits. These general columns are sometimes called *sundry,* or *general ledger,* columns. They are needed for entries affecting accounts for which special columns have not been provided. Column headings ordinarily do not appear in a two-column journal, but they are needed when special columns are used, in order to avoid confusion.

In appearance the columnar general journal may be similar to the two-column journal with added space for the special columns, but there is no standard form.

Entries in the Columnar General Journal. Transactions may be journalized in a columnar general journal with a separate line for each debit and credit item, as in the two-column form, but space can be saved by using only one line for those entries which use the special columns.

The following example shows how an entry may be made on one line to journalize the purchase of an office chair for five dollars cash: (1) Place the date in the date column; (2) in the column for account names, write the name of the account to be debited—Office Equipment—since presumably there is no special column for this account; (3) in the column for explanations, and on the same line if there is room enough, write a brief explanation of the transaction, such as "chair from X Co."; (4) in the column for miscellaneous debits, enter the amount, $5.00; and (5) enter the same amount on the same line in the column for cash credits. In this manner a journal entry is made on one line, whereas it would require at least three lines in a two-column journal: one each for the debit, the credit, and the explanation. It was not necessary to write the name of the cash account, because the item will be posted later to the credit side of the cash account as part of the total of the column for cash credits.

Combined Cash Journal. Small enterprises, if they have simple bookkeeping requirements, sometimes confine all of their journalizing to one columnar general journal. They might use a simple two-column journal, but the addition of special columns usually promotes efficiency. Cash transactions occur so frequently that, in the absence of separate journals for cash, the columnar general journal is almost certain to have special columns for cash debits and for cash credits. This book is merely a general journal in which to record all transactions, but because of the importance of the cash transactions it is often called the combined cash journal.[2] This is the type of book in which the journal entry described above is made. It is practical only when there are few transactions to record.

Account Type of Journal. A book which combines the functions of a journal and a ledger is sometimes used in a small business or for personal records. Special columns in this *account type of journal* take the place of a few or all of the ledger accounts which ordinarily would appear in a ledger. Balances are carried forward so that the account columns contain all of the information needed in an account, including, at the end of an accounting period, the necessary totals and balances for the financial statements. This form of *journal-ledger*, or *synoptic journal*, is practical only when one journal and a few ledger accounts are a sufficient record.

Columnar Special Journals. When special journals are used, they provide an initial segregation of transactions by types according to the kind of journal. This is true whether the journal has one amount column or many. A cash disbursements journal, for instance, will contain a record of transactions involving cash credits. The corresponding debits may then be subdivided into classes of entries by using a special column for each important class. Additional columns may be provided for crediting accounts other than cash, for example, Purchase Discount.

Columnar Ledger Accounts. A columnar ledger account is an analytical type of account which supplies the information given by an ordinary ledger account, and, in addition, contains amount columns in which to distribute by classes the items that make up the account. The additional columns provide an analysis of the account.

---

2 The columnar general journal has various titles, such as cash journal, combined cash journal, combination journal, cash book and journal, or simply the journal. When there are special cash journals, the general journal does not contain a record of cash transactions, and should not have the term *cash* in its title.

A ledger account may contain several kinds of information which are properly combined for the sake of simplicity, or for some other good reason. If it should be desirable to segregate this information by classes, a separate general ledger account may be opened for each class. Another way to accomplish this purpose would be the use of a controlling account in the general ledger accompanied by subsidiary accounts in a separate ledger. When there are only a few classes of items, the use of columnar ledger accounts offers a third method, providing another application of the controlling account. This method has found increasing favor in recent years.

A columnar ledger account combines on one bookkeeping form the functions of a controlling account and a subsidiary ledger. Two columns ordinarily contain postings for the entire account. They constitute a controlling account for the remaining columns, each of which is the equivalent of an account in a subsidiary ledger.

SPECIAL JOURNALS

A special journal is a book of original entry in which are segregated specific types of transactions similar in nature in that they have a like effect on a particular account.[3] It is a labor-saving device designed to increase bookkeeping efficiency. It is especially useful where large numbers of transactions occur which can be segregated into classes so that group totals, instead of individual items, may be posted.

Special journals can provide space for a large proportion of the entries that would otherwise have to be made in the general journal, and thus they reduce the bulk of the general journal. They also permit more clerks to work on the books at one time than would be possible if only one journal were used.

---

3 A special journal may be known by such terms as journal, book, register, or record.

Kinds of Special Journals. A few types of transactions occur so frequently that they have brought about the wide-spread use of four special journals to supplement the general journal, as follows:

1. Cash receipts journal
2.. Cash disbursements journal
3. Purchases journal
4. Sales journal.

Sometimes all cash transactions are journalized in one book, known as the *cash book,* which is a combination of the cash receipts journal and the cash disbursements journal. The cash book often shows the cash receipts and disbursements on opposite pages, the cash receipts being entered on the left-hand page and the cash disbursements on the right-hand page.

Many other journals, such as the voucher register, sales returns and allowances book, notes receivable register, finished goods record, and requisition journal, may be desirable where the transactions which they record occur in sufficient volume.

A private journal is a special journal in which is recorded information that the management considers confidential and desires for some reason to withhold from the accounting department. Such information may deal with matters like officers' accounts or amounts of salaries. The private journal is used infrequently and is usually accompanied by a private ledger.

Forms of Special Journals. A wide variation in the number and arrangement of columns in a special journal is possible, depending largely upon the convenience and preference of those who use the books. There may be any number of debit and credit columns, arranged in any order. Date, explanation, and folio columns may also appear in any order. A column heading should make clear the purpose of each column. As in the case of the general journal, a large number of columns will make a special journal unwieldy, and will increase the possibility of entering an amount in the wrong column.

Single-column Special Journals. Perhaps the simplest form of special journals is the single-column form. This type of journal has only one money column. The first column ordinarily contains the date, the second shows for each transaction the name of the account not provided for by an amount column, the third is used for necessary details explaining the transaction, the fourth is the ledger folio column, and the fifth column is the money, or amount, column.

This form may be used only when all of the transactions it records affect one account in the same manner, either to debit it or to credit it. A sales book, for example, may be a single-column journal. Only sales will be journalized in it. Periodically, probably at the end of each month, the one money column is totaled and the amount posted to the credit side of the sales account. Debit items are posted individually to their several accounts, and the sum of all the separate debit postings from the sales journal should equal the one credit to the sales account.

If controlling accounts are used, and if all sales are made to customers on account, only two postings are required periodically to the general ledger from the single-column sales book. The total of the amount column is debited to the accounts receivable controlling account and credited to the sales account. There are relatively few situations in which single-column journals are satisfactory; hence most journals have two or more columns.

Multiple-column Special Journals. Types of transactions which occur frequently enough to justify the use of special journals, usually require further analysis so that business management may have the detailed financial information it needs. Such additional analysis is possible in multiple-column special journals, where special columns similar to those found in a columnar general journal provide for the sub-classification of similar types of items. For instance, the management may desire an analysis of sales by commodities or by departments of the business. Special columns in a multiple-column sales book can supply such information. Cash payments, while always creating a credit to the Cash account, may also require an occasional credit to the Purchase Discount account, as well as debits to the Accounts Payable account and to a variety of expense accounts. Special columns in the cash disbursements book provide a medium for the segregation of these various elements.

Advantages of Special Journals. Some of the advantages of special journals may be summarized as follows:

1. They segregate types of transactions and keep them from being scattered throughout the general journal, thus reducing the bulk of the general journal and simplifying the reference to a particular transaction or to the type as a whole.

2. They save labor, as the grouping of similar transactions and the increased use of special columns minimizes the need for writing account names and explanations in journalizing, and the columnar totals reduce the amount of posting and relieve the ledger of a mass of details.

3. They facilitate the use of controlling accounts and subsidiary ledgers by supplying the necessary totals, as well as details.

4. They reduce errors because of simplified entries and simplified posting.

5. They enable more than one bookkeeper to work on the books at the same time when there is too much work for one person.

6. They facilitate division of labor, distributing the work among the bookkeepers so that each may become proficient by specializing in a few tasks. No time is lost in shifting from one operation to another, and individuals with limited bookkeeping knowledge can readily be trained to handle many of the operations.

7. They help make effective a system of internal check, in which one employee must check the work of another, thus localizing errors and fixing responsibility.

Disadvantages of Special Journals. With an increase in the number of books used, more space for storage is required and there is greater danger of misplacing books. A small concern can overcome these disadvantages to some extent by keeping special journals on loose-leaf forms in the same cover with the general journal, using index tabs to separate them.

General Journal Not Supplanted. Even when special journals are employed to the fullest practicable extent, they do not supplant the general journal. This journal continues to be useful for some types of entries which occur so infrequently that they do not warrant the setting up of special journals. The general journal should contain such entries as: (1) opening entries, (2) entries for unusual transactions, (3) compound entries that cannot be shown in their entirety in a special journal, (4) correcting entries, and (5) adjusting, closing, and post-closing entries.

SPECIAL LEDGERS

Subdivision of the General Ledger. As business units grow in size and complexity, they need more accounts to give them adequate financial records. When the accounts become too numerous to be handled conveniently in one general ledger, it is customary to place some of them in special ledgers. When a group of similar accounts is large enough to justify its segregation in a subsidiary ledger, it is often advantageous to remove the group from the general ledger, and substitute a controlling account in its place. Conversely, when a single general ledger account proves to be inadequate, a group of related detailed accounts may be established to take its place. Instead of placing all of these new accounts in the general ledger, however, one can place them in a subsidiary ledger, retaining the original general ledger account as a controlling account. There is no definite number of accounts needed to justify a separate subsidiary ledger.

Sudsidiary Ledgers. A subsidiary ledger is a ledger which contains a group of related accounts summarized and represented by a controlling account.

Many businesses maintain at least two subsidiary ledgers in addition to the general ledger: one for accounts with customers, which is labeled variously the accounts receivable, sales, or customers' ledger; and one for creditors' accounts, called the accounts payable, purchase, or creditors' ledger. There may be any number of additional subsidiary ledgers, such as expense, capital stock, factory, plant, and private ledgers.

The accounts in a subsidiary ledger are arranged in any order that proves to be most convenient. They may be written on ordinary standard account forms like those in the general ledger, or on a special form planned for that type of account. Some enterprises prepare a file copy of each invoice representing a charge to a customer's account, which copy is inserted in the subsidiary accounts receivable ledger until payment is received, and is then removed to a transfer file. This plan provides a customers' ledger in which the accounts consist of duplicate copies of unpaid invoices. A similar plan may be followed for an accounts payable ledger, in which the accounts consist of a file of unpaid invoices received from creditors.

CONTROLLING ACCOUNTS

A controlling account is an account which contains in summary form the information given in detail by a group of related accounts in a subsidiary ledger. In this way the general ledger can be relieved of a great many details which are made available in subsidiary ledgers. Conversely, if a general ledger account needs further analysis, subsidiary accounts can be set up to furnish the necessary details.

The close relationship between these accounts requires that every item in a subsidiary account must be represented in the controlling account. Every journal entry which affects any subsidiary account must have the same effect on its controlling account, either as a separate posting or as part of a total. At the end of an accounting period the balance in a controlling account must equal the combined balances of the subsidiary accounts which it controls.

Extent of Use of Controlling Accounts. In a small business, accounts receivable and accounts payable are often the only controlling accounts needed, but in a large concern, most of the general ledger accounts may be controlling accounts. Any general ledger account may be made a controlling account simply by establishing a group of subsidiary accounts in which the information contained in the general ledger account is amplified to any extent desired.

Sometimes, if the information desired in support of a controlling account cannot be disclosed adequately with one series of subsidiary accounts, additional accounts subsidiary to the first series may be required. This makes each of the first series of subsidiary accounts an intermediate controlling account, summarizing its section of the second series, and all of the intermediate controlling accounts in the series are summarized in turn in one controlling account in the general ledger. As need arises, one or more accounts in the second series may be subdivided further in the same manner.

Titles and Forms of Controlling Accounts. An account may have a distinctive title to indicate that it is a controlling account, but it does not need one. For instance, the general ledger controlling account for customers' accounts may be called simply Accounts Receivable, or Accounts Receivable—Control, or any other suitable name.[4]

The same form of ruling that is used for other general ledger accounts is commonly employed for controlling accounts. If there are but a few subsidiary accounts, a columnar form of ledger account may be desirable.

SELF-BALANCING SPECIAL LEDGERS

A subsidiary ledger ordinarily contains an excess of debits, or of credits, equal in amount to the balance in the controlling account. Such a ledger can be converted into a self-balancing ledger by the simple expedient of inserting in it a memorandum account and posting totals to it which are just the opposite of all entries posted to the individual accounts.

This balancing account then contains the same kind of summary information that is posted to the controlling account, except that the amounts are on the opposite side of the account.[5] The balances of the two accounts must be the same amount, but one will be a debit and the other a credit. The controlling account and the subsidiary ledger balancing account are often referred to as *reciprocal accounts,* or *interlocking accounts.*

A subsidiary ledger, such as a factory ledger or a branch ledger, which is kept at some distance from the general ledger, may contain a balancing account to assist the book-

4 Other names sometimes given the controlling account for customers' accounts are Accounts Receivable—Controlling account, Accounts Receivable—Trade, Customers' Accounts, Customers' Ledger account, or Trade Debtors. The accounts payable controlling account is given such titles as Accounts Payable, Accounts Payable—Trade Creditors' Accounts, and Trade Creditors.

5 The memorandum balancing account in a subsidiary ledger carries a variety of names, such as General Ledger account, Home Office account, Main Office account, Balancing Account, General Balancing Account, and General Ledger Adjustment account.

keeper in determining readily whether or not his ledger is in balance. Frequently, however, there is no particular advantage in maintaining the self-balancing feature when the ledgers are in the same office, for then the accuracy of the subsidiary ledger totals is readily tested by making an abstract or schedule of them for comparison with the controlling account.

ADVANTAGES OF SUBSIDIARY LEDGERS AND CONTROLLING ACCOUNTS

Subsidiary ledgers, controlling accounts, and special journals have somewhat similar advantages, resulting from the fact that they supplement each other. The principal advantages of special journals are listed earlier in this chapter. Advantages of subsidiary ledgers and controlling accounts are as follows:

1. They segregate types of accounts, and so provide a logical grouping of similar items.

2. They keep down the bulk of the general ledger by substituting a controlling account for a group of accounts, thus shortening the trial balance and simplifying the preparation of financial statements.

3. They provide details and summaries, the subsidiary ledgers containing the individual items which the controlling accounts represent with totals.

4. They reduce errors.

5. They enable more than one bookkeeper to work on the books at one time.

6. They facilitate division of labor.

7. They help make a system of internal check effective.

Since the last four advantages listed above are identical with the last four advantages of special journals, previously listed, they are not explained here.

PROCEDURES WITH SPECIAL JOURNALS
AND SPECIAL LEDGERS

Entries in Columnar Journals. Procedures for recording transactions in special-column journals may be indicated in general terms as follows:

1. Place the date of each transaction in the date column. Some bookkeepers prefer to show the date in the middle of the page just before each entry. Others place it at the top of the page and do not repeat it unless the date changes. When the date column is used, it is desirable to show the year at the top of the column, and the month and day on the line on which the first entry begins. Subsequent entries may include the month and day, the day only, or no date if it is the same as the preceding entry.

2. In the column for account names, place the name of any general ledger account to be debited if there is no special column for this account. If there are several such debits, use a separate line for each.

3. Place the amount for each of the foregoing accounts in the column for miscellaneous debits on the line bearing the name of the account to be debited.

4. On the next line, directly beneath the last name in the account names column, write the name of any general ledger account to be credited, if there is no special column, for this account.

5. Write the amount of the credit for the foregoing account on the same line in the column for miscellaneous credits.

6. If either a debit or a credit item belongs in a special column, place it there, and in the column for account names give the name of the subsidiary account involved, if any. It is not necessary to write the name

of the general ledger account affected, since this name appears at the head of the special column in which the item is entered. Items in special columns can be placed on the same line with other items to save space, except when a separate line is necessary for proper identification in the account names column.

7.   Write a brief explanation in the column for explanations, unless the transaction was so simple and so common that no further details will be needed in the future to support this entry. Sometimes there is only one column for account names and explanations. Then the explanation may be written across the entire column, beginning on the line below the rest of the entry, as in the two-column general journal. In order to save space it may be written at the right side of the account name, in the same column, and on the same line.

8.   Write nothing in the folio column, ordinarily, until later, when the items are posted to the ledger accounts.

The instructions given above (except number 6) apply to transactions recorded in the miscellaneous, or sundry, columns. Many of the entries in a columnar journal appear in the special columns, however. These entries record transactions which tend to be relatively simple and occur frequently, so that they require a minimum of explanation and usually only one line each in the journal.

It should be noted that the general journal always requires two sundry columns, one for debits and one for credits, so that any kind of transaction can be recorded in it. A special journal limits the kinds of transactions it records, and for that reason needs only one sundry column, ordinarily, or none at all.

Proving the Journal. In order to be sure that the debits and credits in a journal are equal, the journal should be *proved,* by footing the amount columns and seeing that the sum of the debit column totals agrees with the sum of the credit column totals. It is not necessary to write the totals in a two-column general column, where each item is posted separately. When more columns are used, however, most of them require totals for posting purposes, and it is customary to show the totals for all of them as an aid in proving the journal.

It is desirable to write the totals at the bottom of each page, and carry them forward to the proper columns at the top of the next page, so that the equality of the debits and credits can be tested on any page instead of waiting until the end of the accounting period.

Posting to Subsidiary Ledgers. When subsidiary accounts are used, it is customary to have special columns in the journals in which to record transactions affecting such accounts, in order to provide not only the details for the subsidiary accounts, but totals, as well, for the controlling accounts. The details are posted to the subsidiary accounts when convenient, perhaps daily, in order to keep the accounts up to date. The column totals are posted to the controlling accounts only at monthly or other infrequent intervals.

When posting to subsidiary accounts from a special column in a journal, the bookkeeper obtains the amount from the special column and the name of the account from the column for account names. He enters in the account the date of the transaction, the journal page on which it is recorded, the amount, and, if considered necessary, a very brief description. He places the ledger page number, or the account number, in the folio column in the journal on the line containing the item posted. If neither the ledger pages nor the accounts are numbered, a check mark placed in the folio column in the journal indicates a completed posting.

---

6 Some bookkeepers prefer to place the account numbers in the journal when journalizing, so that the accounts may be found more readily when posting. After an item has been posted, a check mark is placed in the journal beside the account number or beside the amount.

It is possible at times to improve the bookkeeping procedures by journalizing groups of transactions in summary form instead of making a separate journal entry for each individual transaction. For example, the duplicate copies of invoices representing sales to customers on account, may be totaled and recorded periodically, perhaps daily or monthly, so that one journal entry covers many sales. Under such a plan, posting to the individual subsidiary accounts with customers cannot be made from the journal, which has a record of the transactions only in summary form. These postings will be made directly from the duplicate invoices and may be made before the journal entry is recorded.

Sometimes an item affecting a subsidiary account appears in the sundry debits column or the sundry credits column of a journal because there is no special column for it. Such an item will be posted to the subsidiary account in the same manner as if it were journalized in a special column. It will also be posted to the controlling account as an individual item, and special care must be exercised in order to be sure that both postings are made.

Posting from Columnar Journals to the General Ledger. Ordinarily a special-column journal has a column for sundry debits, or one for sundry credits, or both, containing items for which no special columns are provided. Such items are posted individually to the general ledger accounts in a manner similar to that employed in posting to a subsidiary account. Totals of the sundry columns are never posted, since the items comprising them are posted individually.

Special columns, on the other hand, are posted to the general ledger accounts by totals, never by items. The heading of a special column contains the name of the general ledger account to which the total is to be posted, and indicates whether the items in the column are debits or credits. The date of the entry in the ledger is the date on which the special column was totaled, usually the last day of the month.

A notation at the foot of the column, perhaps inclosed in a circle just below the total, indicates that the total has been posted.

It is important to indicate by a notation in the journal, such as a ledger page number, an account number, or a check mark, that an individual item or a column total has been posted. Thus a glance at a journal page can reveal whether or not all of the items have been posted.

General Ledger in Balance Periodically. Items that appear in the sundry columns of the journals are posted to the general ledger day by day at any convenient time, whereas special columns are totaled and posted only at the close of the month, or at other periodic intervals. The general ledger, therefore, does not balance throughout the period, but only after all of the postings have been made at the end of the period.

Comparison of Subsidiary Ledgers and Controlling Account Balances. Periodically a comparison should be made between the balance of a controlling account and the sum of the balances of the subsidiary accounts which it controls. This is accomplished by listing the subsidiary account balances, the total of which should agree with the balance of the controlling account. When such a list includes the names of the subsidiary accounts, with their balances, it is called a list, an abstract, or a schedule of these accounts.

Transactions Involving Several Journals. Sometimes it is desirable to record all or portions of a transaction in more than one journal in order to utilize special columns. For instance, the bookkeeper may record a cash sale in both the cash receipts book and the sales book. In the cash receipts book, he may enter the amount of the transaction in the special column for cash debits and also in the column for sundry credits, indicating in the column for account names that the sundry credit is a Sales account item. At the same time, he enters the transaction in the sales book, crediting the Sales account in the special column for sales and debiting the Cash account in the sundry debits column. He then places a check mark in both journals in the folio columns to indicate that the sundry items are not to be posted. Thus there will be only one cash debit for the transaction, and it will reach the ledger as part of the total of the special column for cash debits in the cash receipts book. There will be only one sales credit, which will be part of the total of the sales column in the sales book.

This method of preventing double posting, by checking duplicate entries in the journals, is known as *blank checking,* or *cross checking.*

ADDITIONAL BIBLIOGRAPHY*

Bolon, Dallas S., *Introduction to Accounting,* 2nd ed. New York: John Wiley & Sons, Inc., 1938. Pp. 121-175.

Cole, Dana F., *Beginning Accounting.* New York: Thomas Y. Crowell Co., 1940. Pp. 229-275.

Elwell, Fayette H., *Elementary Accounting.* Boston: Ginn and Co., 1945. Pp. 55-67, 289-315, 332-347.

Hatfield, Henry R., Sanders, Thomas H., and Burton, Norman L., *Accounting Principles and Practices.* Boston: Ginn and Co., 1940. Pp. 157-184.

Howard, Stanley E., *The A B C of Accounting,* 3rd ed. Princeton: Princeton University Press, 1938. Pp. 107-123.

Kelley, Arthur C., *Essentials of Accounting.* New York: American Book Co., 1935. Pp. 133-146, 162-174, 288-289.

Kennedy, Donald D., Esterly, George R., and von Minden, William J., *Introductory Accounting.* New York: The Ronald Press Co., 1942. Pp. 252-352.

Lamberton, Robert A., *Fundamentals of Accounting.* New York: Longmans, Green and Co., 1942. Pp. 115-151, 348-359.

Prickett, Alva L., and Mikesell, R. Merrill, *Principles of Accounting,* rev. ed. New York: The Macmillan Co. 1937. Pp. 93-106, 184-206.

Rorem, C. Rufus, *Accounting Method,* 2nd ed. Chicago: The University of Chicago Press, 1930. Pp. 175-219.

Scoville, Hiram T., and Moyer, C. A., *Fundamentals of Accounting.* Boston: D. C. Heath and Co., 1940. Pp. 167-236, 387-416.

---

* For other references, see the QUICK REFERENCE TABLE TO STANDARD TEXTBOOKS in the forepart of this book.

VIII

Auxiliary Records

THE USE OF AUXILIARY RECORDS

Auxiliary records are those records which are maintained by an enterprise in addition to the journals and ledgers. They are supplementary records. They provide management with additional detailed information which cannot be given conveniently or economically in the basic journals and ledgers.

The designation is merely one of convenience, as the distinction between auxiliary records and the basic books is not a fundamental one. Their fields often overlap. Sometimes an auxiliary record takes the place of a special journal or performs the function of a subsidiary ledger. Many kinds of auxiliary records are used. The types found most frequently can be classified as registers and sundry business papers.

REGISTERS

A register is a type of record which usually supplements the information given in the journals and ledgers, but which also in some instances serves as a special journal or as a subsidiary ledger. Its form varies according to the purpose for which it is maintained. Frequently it is a columnar form.

Registers for notes receivable, notes payable, and insurance policies are examples of auxiliary records which supplement the information contained in the journals and ledgers. Such registers may provide the details necessary to journalize the transactions and also additional information desired by the management. The notes receivable and notes payable registers show the data which would be included in the journal and also such additional information as due date, date of payment, and interest rate. The insurance policy register provides such information as date of policy, policy number, name of insurance company, property insured, amount of policy, amount of unexpired premium both at the beginning and at the close of the fiscal year, and the amount of the expired premium at the close of the year.

A register often is employed in connection with business papers which are numbered serially. It provides a summarized record of the information contained in the papers and also a control over the papers used, since every one must be accounted for even though some may be voided, or cancelled, because of errors.

A register may be a book of original entry from which postings are made. It is then a special journal. Examples of this kind of register are the sales register, the check register, and the voucher register. The papers recorded in each of these customarily bear serial numbers. The sales register takes the place of the sales journal, the check register takes the place of the cash disbursements journal, and the voucher register takes the place of the purchases journal.

In some instances registers serve as subsidiary ledgers. For example, a fixed assets register can supply all of the details needed in support of controlling accounts for Machinery and for Reserve for Depreciation of Machinery when it is kept in such a manner that it shows the date of acquisition and cost of each machine, with name of maker and serial number, estimated useful life, estimated final trade-in or scrap value, depreciation computed in previous years, and the monthly charges for depreciation during the current fiscal year.

BUSINESS PAPERS

Business papers, sometimes called vouchers, supporting documents, or underlying documents, consist of any written matter in addition to the journals and ledgers which may be used as evidence supporting a business transaction. They assist the accounting department in proving the accuracy of its records. At the time a transaction takes place, some written record is usually made which lessens the danger of errors and of future misunderstandings between the parties involved.

Business papers are important for the following reasons:

1. They constitute the original data upon which many of the book entries are based.

2. They aid the system of internal check.

3. They are useful for reference and verification.

4. They form a basis for income tax, social security and payroll tax, and other government reports.

5. They may be a factor in settling legal controversies, sometimes being considered more important as evidence than the journals and ledgers which have been prepared from them.

CLASSIFICATION OF BUSINESS PAPERS

The following is a classified list of some of the more important business papers, described briefly.

Papers Relating to Purchases.

1. Purchase requisition, initiating the purchase by indicating need for commodities

2. Purchase order, requesting the vendor to ship goods

3. Purchase invoice, prepared by the vendor for the purchaser, usually showing a list of goods shipped together with prices and terms

4. Credit memorandum, issued by the vendor, reducing the amount owed by the purchaser

5. Voucher, authorizing entry in the voucher register to record purchase of commodities or services, and, at the proper time, authorizing payment by check.

Papers Relating to Sales.

1. Sales ticket, or slip, giving the detailed information concerning a retail sale

2. Sales invoice, prepared by the vendor, giving the details of a retail sale by mail or a sale by manufacturer, wholesaler, or jobber

3. Credit memorandum, prepared by the vendor, reducing the amount owed to him

4. Bill of lading, relating to a freight shipment

5. Statement of account, indicating the status of the account with the purchaser and sometimes aiding in the collection of the amount due.

Papers Relating to Cash Receipts.

1. Cash sales ticket, giving the details of a cash sale

2. Cash register tape, listing briefly the cash transactions

3. Receipt issued to the payer, acknowledging cash received

4. Correspondence concerning cash received by the enterprise.

Papers Relating to Cash Disbursements.

1. Check, used for making payment, together with the carbon copy or check stub

2. Remittance advice, describing the purpose of the payment

3. Voucher, authorizing payment by check

4. Petty cash voucher, explaining small payment in cash, described later in the chapter

5. Receipt for cash paid out.

Papers Relating to Bank Transactions.

1. Signature card, furnishing the bank with the signature which the depositor will use in signing checks

2. Deposit ticket, or deposit slip, a form accompanying a bank deposit and listing the items deposited

3. Pass book, a small book in which the bank enters the amount of each deposit as a receipt for the depositor

4. Check book, a book of detachable blank checks, usually with stubs, providing the depositor with convenient forms for making withdrawals and a memorandum record of the bank account

5. Debit or credit memorandum, prepared by the bank to adjust the bank account

6. Bank statement, usually a periodic statement for the depositor, showing the deposits, withdrawals, and balance of his account

7. Bank reconciliation, described later in the chapter, prepared and used by the depositor to compare the bank statement with his record of the account.

Negotiable Instruments.

1. Draft, a bill of exchange, signed by the drawer, requesting the drawee, usually a debtor, to make payment according to the stated terms—for example, a bank check, certified check, travelers check, bank draft, commercial draft, and trade acceptance

2. Cashier's check, drawn by a bank upon itself

3. Express money order, payable at an express company office

4. Postal money order, payable at a Post Office

5. Promissory note, an unconditional written promise, made by one person to another, signed by the maker, engaging to pay on demand or at a fixed or determinable future time, to order or to bearer, a certain sum of money

6. Bond, as defined in Chapter XII, negotiable if not registered

7. Warehouse receipt, showing that goods purchased have been stored, title to which may be transferred by transferring the receipt

8. Bill of lading, a written contract in which the carrier acknowledges receipt of goods and agrees to transport them.

Miscellaneous Business Papers.

1. Ordinary correspondence, contracts, insurance policies, deeds, licenses, inventory sheets, expense bills, mortgages, receipts, statistical reports, letters of credit, etc.

2. Journal voucher, an office form required in some enterprises as the authority for each journal entry.

BANK RECONCILIATION

A business enterprise which maintains one or more bank accounts ordinarily prepares a bank reconciliation at the close of each month. This is done in order to make a comparison between the bank statement and the depositor's records, and to account for any differences between them. Either the bank or the depositor may have made an error due to an omission or to mathematical inaccuracy. If the error has been made by the depositor, he should know about it, locate it, and correct his records. If the error has been made by the bank, it should be notified in order that proper corrections may be made there.

The reconciliation is made by checking the withdrawals as shown on the bank statement against the canceled checks returned, the check stubs, or the check register, and the deposits against the duplicate deposit slips or the cash receipts journal. This permits the ready identification of checks drawn but not yet paid and deposits sent to the bank but not yet credited to the account at the reconcilation date. A memorandum record of the reconciliation should be made. It may be prepared by listing first, the balance as shown by the bank statement, then listing the outstanding checks and subtracting their total from the balance and adding deposits for which credit has not yet been given. If there are other differences, they should be noted. The resulting figure should be the same as the balance shown by the check stubs and the cash account.

PETTY CASH

It is generally conceded that a strict accounting for all cash transactions can be obtained more readily if all cash received is deposited in a bank, and all disbursements are made by check. Nevertheless, numerous small expenditures must be made from time to time in the average business office for such items as postage stamps, express charges, and messenger service. These expenditures can be made more conveniently with cash than with checks.

The imprest system for handling a *petty cash fund* provides a plan for making minor payments with cash and later repaying the amounts to the fund by check, so that the books will show checks issued for all disbursements. Petty cash expenditures are recorded in the ledger accounts only at intervals, when replenishing checks are issued to cover them.

A petty cash fund is established by drawing and cashing a check, and debiting Petty Cash and crediting Cash with the amount. This cash is kept in a petty cash box, or drawer, separate from incoming cash, and a record of payments from it is maintained in a petty cash book. When a payment is made, the cashier must obtain a receipt for it. Such a receipt, which is necessary to support the petty cash records, is usually called a *petty cash voucher*. The petty cash fund is replenished periodically, or when the cash remaining on hand reaches a predetermined minimum. To replenish the fund, a check is issued for the amount necessary to bring the cash up to the original figure, and petty cash vouchers for that amount are filed as underlying documents supporting the records.

The amount of a replenishing check is debited to the accounts affected, as shown by the petty cash book, and Cash account is credited without affecting the Petty Cash account, according to one method of accounting for petty cash expenditures. No entries are made in the Petty Cash account under this method except when a change in policy requires an increase or decrease in the petty cash fund. The amount of this fund remains constant, and must at all times be equalled by the total petty cash and petty cash vouchers on hand.

Under another method of accounting for petty cash expenditures, the amount of the check replenishing the fund is debited to Petty Cash account and credited to Cash. At the same time, Petty Cash account is credited with the same amount and the individual accounts affected by the petty cash payments, as shown by the petty cash book, are debited. Thus the Petty Cash account reflects the total amounts paid out of the fund and the dates on which replenishing checks were issued, but the amount of the fund does not change.

ADDITIONAL BIBLIOGRAPHY*

Bolon, Dallas S., *Introduction to Accounting,* 2nd ed. New York: John Wiley & Sons, Inc., 1938. Pp. 20-27, 370-389.

Cole, Dana F., *Beginning Accounting.* New York: Thomas Y. Crowell Co., 1940. Pp. 637-650, 662-663, Appendix 1-64.

Elwell, Fayette H., *Elementary Accounting.* Boston: Ginn and Co., 1945. Pp. 128-184, 335-340, 665-696.

Hatfield, Henry R., Sanders, Thomas H., and Burton, Norman L., *Accounting Principles and Practices.* Boston: Ginn and Co., 1940. Pp. 196-218.

Jackson, J. Hugh, *Accounting Principles.* Los Angeles: Charles R. Hadley Co., 1944. Pp. 121-180, 213-246.

Kelley, Arthur C., *Essentials of Accounting.* New York: American Book Co., 1935. Pp. 86-102, 147-159.

Kennedy, Donald D., Esterly, George R., and von Minden, William J., *Introductory Accounting.* New York: The Ronald Press Co., 1942. Pp. 192-230.

Lamberton, Robert A., *Fundamentals of Accounting.* New York: Longmans, Green and Co., 1942. Pp. 73-86, 92-114.

Prickett, Alva L., and Mikesell, R. Merrill, *Principles of Accounting,* rev. ed. New York: The Macmillan Co., 1937. Pp. 227-245.

Rorem, C. Rufus, *Accounting Method,* 2nd ed. Chicago: The University of Chicago Press, 1930. Pp. 220-237.

Scovill, Hiram T., and Moyer, C. A., *Fundamentals of Accounting.* Boston: D. C. Heath and Co., 1940. Pp. 305-332, 423-468, 491-561.

---

* For other references, see the QUICK REFERENCE TABLE TO STANDARD TEXTBOOKS in the forepart of this book.

The Voucher System

The voucher system is the part of the accounting system of many enterprises which provides for the verification and prompt recording of all transactions involving expenditures, and the authorization of such expenditures. Petty cash payments are an apparent exception to this procedure, but when a check is issued to replenish the petty cash fund, it must pass through the same routine as other checks, including verification and approval of the items covered and authorization of the check's issuance.

In some enterprises the voucher system is not required to include all transactions which involve expenditures. For example, a check may be drawn for an occasional disbursement, such as the payment of a note payable or the purchase of an asset, without a voucher to authorize it. Such departures from a rigid adherence to the voucher system render its control less effective.

Part of the value of the voucher system lies in the fact that it is one of the most important factors in an efficient method of internal check, especially in controlling expenditures.

THE VOUCHER

As used in the voucher system, a voucher may be defined as a paper on which a transaction involving an expenditure is summarized, and signatures or other marks appear which vouch for its correctness, authorize its entry in the books, and approve its payment at the proper time.[1] Under the voucher system, no check should be issued unless it is authorized by a voucher.

Form of the Voucher. The form of a voucher varies considerably in different businesses, and there is much variation in the amount of information required on a voucher, but certain common characteristics may be noted. A printed form is generally used. A simple form may be printed on one side only. If it is printed on both sides and is to be folded, the front may show an explanation of the transaction together with the signatures or initials to provide the necessary authorization, while the back shows the accounts to be debited, and the inside contains detailed information relative to the transaction. This information on the inside of the voucher will be similar to that contained in the invoice. It will give such data as the following: name of creditor; date of purchase; terms; date payment is due, both with and without the discount; net amount payable; a brief description of the transaction; and spaces to show payment date and check number.

A single copy of a voucher is sufficient in some offices. In others the voucher is prepared with one or more carbon copies to be filed so as to facilitate cross reference. For instance, the original may be filed numerically according to the voucher number, one copy alphabetically according to the vendor's name, and another copy according to the payment date.

The Voucher Check. A voucher check is a form of voucher and check combined. It contains information, either on the check itself or on a detachable slip, indicating to the payee the purpose for which the check was issued. The check and the voucher are prepared at the same time, but

---

1 Any business paper may be called a voucher, as indicated in the preceding chapter; therefore, some writers prefer a distinctive title for the vouchers used in the voucher system, such as accounts payable voucher, formal voucher, or cash voucher.

usually the check is not dated, signed, or numbered until authority is given to send it to the payee. The voucher is merely a carbon copy of the check and accompanying information, with the addition of any desired details, such as journalizing instructions and approval signatures.

Preparation of a Voucher. Vouchers should be prepared promptly in order to keep the records up to date. Attached to a voucher will be the necessary documents relating to the transaction to be recorded. As the voucher is sent from department to department, each person charged with a responsibility regarding it will make necessary notations on it, initial it, and send it on to the next department in keeping with the established routine. This makes available in one place all the necessary information relative to a particular transaction, and fixes a definite responsibility on each one who has made notations on the voucher.

THE VOUCHER REGISTER

A voucher register is a special journal in which the vouchers are entered, and also a subsidiary ledger showing the unpaid amounts owing to creditors.

The Voucher Register a Journal. The voucher register is an expanded form of the purchases journal, recording transactions relating not only to the purchases of merchandise for resale, as does the purchases journal, but also including all other transactions concerned with the acquisition of assets and services, or in any way connected with the disbursement of cash. When a voucher register is used. the check register becomes a simple record, since all checks are recorded with debits to one account only, the Vouchers Payable account, and credits to Cash, with occasional credits to Purchase Discounts.

Form of the Voucher Register. Voucher registers, as well as vouchers, vary considerably in form. Like the voucher, the voucher register is designed to meet the requirements of the particular business in which it will be used. It is usually ruled with separate columns for each of the following: date of voucher, name of creditor, explanation and terms, voucher number, date of payment, check number, an amount column for credits to Vouchers Payable (or Audited Vouchers Payable, or Accounts Payable), and such debit columns as are needed to classify and distribute the expenditures, including an amount column for debits to sundry accounts for which no special columns are provided, and a column for the names of such accounts.

Recording a Voucher. After each voucher has been prepared and its entry properly authorized, it is recorded in the voucher register in its numerical order. It is then placed in the unpaid vouchers file, unless it is to be paid at once. When authorization is given for the payment of a newly made voucher, or an older one that is already in the unpaid file, a check is drawn according to the information on the voucher. If a voucher check is used, the previously written check is dated, numbered, and signed. The check is entered in the check register, and the date and number are placed in the voucher register on the line recording the voucher to indicate its payment, while the voucher is removed to the paid vouchers file.

Posting from the Voucher Register. Items in the voucher register are posted to the general ledger periodically, usually monthly, except sundry debits, which are posted at any convenient time. All columns are totaled, as in any columnar journal, and the equality of total debits and total credits is proved. Then the total of each special column is posted to the account indicated in the column heading, and any unposted items in the column for sundry debits are posted individually to the accounts designated in the column for account names.

The Voucher Register a Ledger. The voucher register supplants the accounts payable ledger, and thus possesses

the attributes of a subsidiary ledger in addition to the previously mentioned journal characteristics. A separate creditors' ledger may be maintained as part of a voucher system,
if desired, but the voucher register makes this unnecessary
by showing at all times the unpaid amounts still owing to
creditors. Such amounts appear in the voucher register as
a record of the individual vouchers, arranged in their
numerical order, and there may be several amounts owing
to the same creditor on different transactions. On the other
hand, the accounts in the creditors' ledger give a cumulative
history of the transactions with each creditor, in alphabetical
or other desired sequence. Extra effort and expense are
required to keep a creditors' ledger, however, and the
voucher register is considered to be an ample record by
many enterprises, especially if bills are paid promptly so
that a list of the unpaid vouchers can be prepared readily.

Abstract of Vouchers Payable. The voucher register
provides a ready reference to the vouchers themselves, and
maintains a control over the file of unpaid vouchers, since
the total amount of vouchers listed in the voucher register
for which no payment date or check number is shown,
should agree with the total amount of the vouchers in the
unpaid vouchers file.

Periodically, usually at the end of each month, an abstract
of vouchers payable is prepared by listing the unpaid vouchers as shown in the voucher register. This list, or schedule,
should agree with the vouchers in the unpaid vouchers file.
An alternative procedure for the preparation of the abstract is to list the vouchers in the unpaid vouchers file, and
compare the list with the unpaid vouchers according to the
voucher register. The total of the abstract must agree with
the balance in the Vouchers Payable controlling account in
the general ledger.

ADDITIONAL BIBLIOGRAPHY*

Bolon, Dallas S., *Introduction to Accounting*, 2nd ed. New York: John Wiley & Sons, Inc., 1938. Pp. 390-402.

Cole, Dana F., *Beginning Accounting*. New York: Thomas Y. Crowell Co., 1940. Pp. 275-283.

Elwell, Fayette H., *Elementary Accounting*. Boston: Ginn and Co., 1945. Pp. 369-379.

Hatfield, Henry R., Sanders, Thomas H., and Burton, Norman L., *Accounting Principles and Practices*. Boston: Ginn and Co., 1940. Pp. 185-195.

Jackson, J. Hugh, *Accounting Principles*. Los Angeles: Charles R. Hadley Co., 1944. Pp. 563-579.

Kelley, Arthur C., *Essentials of Accounting*. New York: American Book Co., 1935. Pp. 288-317.

Kennedy, Donald D., Esterly, George R., and von Minden, William J., *Introductory Accounting*. New York: The Ronald Press Co., 1942. P. 252.

Lamberton, Robert A., *Fundamentals of Accounting*. New York: Longmans, Green and Co., 1942. Pp. 390-409.

Prickett, Alva L., and Mikesell, R. Merrill, *Principles of Accounting*, rev. ed. New York: The Macmillan Co., 1937. Pp. 207-226.

Rorem, C Rufus, *Accounting Method*, 2nd ed. Chicago: The University of Chicago Press, 1930. Pp. 223-227.

Scovill, Hiram T., and Moyer, C. A., *Fundamentals of Accounting*. Boston: D. C. Heath and Co., 1940. Pp. 469-490.

---

* For other references, see the QUICK REFERENCE TABLE TO STANDARD TEXTBOOKS in the forepart of this book.

Single Proprietorship — Partnership

There are three principal types of business organization, the *single proprietorship,* the *partnership,* and the *corporation.* These differ in structure and in the legal technicalities affecting their formation and subsequent actions. Each type has similar accounting requirements relating to the assets and liabilities, but uses distinctive proprietary accounts. This chapter discusses the single proprietorship and the partnership. The following chapter discusses the corporation.

SINGLE PROPRIETORSHIP

The simplest form of business organization is the single proprietorship, sometimes called sole proprietorship or individual proprietorship. In this type of organization, a single proprietor owns the business and is responsible for its operation. The proprietor is entitled to the profits that are made and must bear the losses, if they occur.

Advantages of the Single Proprietorship. The principal advantages enjoyed by the single proprietorship over other forms of business organization are:

1. Ease of formation—less formality and fewer legal restrictions than for the establishment of other forms

2. Sole ownership of profits—proprietor not required to share profits with anyone

3. Control vested in one owner—no co-owners to consult

4. Flexibility—no permission necessary from the state for performance of any legal act

5. Relative freedom from government control and special taxation.

Disadvantages of the Single Proprietorship.

1. Unlimited liability—individual proprietor responsible for full amount of debts of his business even though they may exceed his investment

2. Unstable life—enterprise automatically terminated upon death of owner or his disposal of the business

3. Less capital available, ordinarily, than in other types of business organization

4. Difficulty of obtaining long-term loans

5. Narrow viewpoint and limited experience more probable with one owner than with several.

PROPRIETARY ACCOUNTS

In the single proprietorship, two accounts are ordinarily kept for the owner. One is his *Capital* account and the other his *Personal*, or *Drawing*, or *Current*, account. It is customary to treat the Personal account as a temporary account, to be closed into the Capital account at the end of the year.

The Capital account is credited with the amount of the original investment, subsequent additional investments, a credit balance transferred from the Personal account, and adjustments, if needed. It is debited with the amount of any permanent withdrawal of investment, a debit balance transferred from the Personal account, and adjustments, if needed. Unless the liabilities of the enterprise exceed the assets, the Capital account should have a credit balance showing the amount of investment.

The Personal account is credited with more or less temporary additions of money, merchandise, and other assets, and with a credit balance from the Profit and Loss account. It is debited with withdrawals of money, merchandise, or other assets in relatively small amounts considered to be in anticipation of profits as contrasted with withdrawals of investment, and with a debit balance of the Profit and Loss account.

DISPOSITION OF PROFIT AND LOSS

A sole proprietor may withdraw his profits as he sees fit. Generally, he takes them in the form of cash or merchandise, debiting the amounts to his Personal account.

The Profit and Loss account, which indicates a profit if it has a credit balance and a loss if it has a debit balance, may be closed to the Personal account, as indicated above. In some enterprises the balance of the Profit and Loss account is closed to the proprietor's Capital account.

PARTNERSHIP

The Uniform Partnership Act, adopted by various states, defines the partnership as "an association of two or more persons to carry on as co-owners a business for profit." A contractual relationship exists between the partners. Some of the characteristics that distinguish a partnership from other forms of business organization are as follows: limited life, unlimited liability of at least one partner, co-ownership of assets, mutual agency, share in management, and share in partnership profits.

Advantages of the Partnership.

1. Ease of formation—legal formalities few compared with requirements for creation of a corporation

2. Direct rewards—partners motivated by direct sharing of profits to apply their best abilities

3. Growth facilitated—more capital and better range of ability possible than in a single proprietorship

4. Flexibility—a partnership may perform any legal act without permission from the state

5. Relative freedom from government control and special taxation.

Disadvantages of the Partnership.

1. Unlimited liability for at least one partner

2. Unstable life

3. Difficulty of obtaining capital in large amounts, particularly through long-term loans

4. Firm bound by acts of one partner as an agent

5. Difficulty of disposing of partnership interest.

FORMATION OF THE PARTNERSHIP

A partnership is ordinarily formed by a voluntary contract between the parties, the contract being either written or oral. To prevent misunderstanding among the partners, it is desirable that such a contract be in writing, in which case the agreement is usually called the articles of copartnership. It is desirable that such an agreement contain considerable detail relative to the relationship between the partners. It is particularly important that matters relating to the ratio in which profits and losses are shared, the investments, the withdrawals, and the rights and duties of the partners should be made part of such an agreement.

LEGAL PROBLEMS OF THE PARTNERSHIP

The relationship between partners gives rise to legal problems not found in other types of business organization. In the eyes of the law, a partnership is an association of individuals, and not an entity like the corporation. Ordinarily, legal actions must involve the individuals rather than the firm.

The relationship of mutual agency gives each partner the right to act as agent for all partners, and to bind them by any acts which would reasonably appear to be within the scope of his authority. Each member of a partnership is individually liable for the debts of the firm except in the cases of limited partnerships, and even in such an instance at least one partner must have unlimited liability.

KINDS OF PARTNERS

The legal status of partners varies not only among partnerships but sometimes among the partners in the same enterprise. Some of the more common classes of partners are as follows:

1. General partner. A general partner is liable to an unlimited extent for the partnership debts and has a voice in the management.

2. Limited partner. A limited, or special, partner is liable to a limited extent for the partnership debts. An individual can have the status of a limited partner only under the restricted conditions expressly permitted by law.

3. Silent partner

4. Secret partner

5. Dormant partner

6. Nominal partner

7. Ostensible partner

8. Junior partner.

ADMISSION OF A NEW PARTNER

A new partnership results when an additional partner joins a partnership. The same accounting records may be continued, or new books may be required. There are two bases for the admission of a new partner, one representing the purchase of a part of existing partnership interests, and the other representing the investment of additional assets in the business. In either case the accounting problem involved is to record the partners' capital accounts correctly.

The ways in which a new partner is admitted may be listed as follows:

Purchase of a Part of Existing Partnership Interests. An incoming partner may purchase his interest from one or more of the old partners, paying them directly without affecting the assets of the partnership. Regardless of the actual size of his investment, his capital account is credited with an amount agreed upon which is deducted from the capital accounts of one or more of the old partners.

Investment of Additional Assets in the Enterprise. When the amount invested by an incoming partner is placed in the partnership, the assets of the enterprise will be increased by at least the amount of the investment. Following are five bases for recording the investment of such additional assets in the enterprise:

1. *Goodwill allowance to old partners.* Goodwill created by the old partnership is recorded by debiting Goodwill account and crediting the capital accounts of the old partners.

2. *Goodwill allowance to new partner.* Goodwill brought to the enterprise by the new partner is recorded by debiting Goodwill account and crediting the capital account of the new partner.

3. *Bonus to old partners.* Goodwill created by the old partnership is not recorded as an asset. The investment of the new partner is recorded by debiting assets for the total amount, crediting the old partners' capital accounts with the amount of the bonus, and crediting the new partner's capital account with the balance.

4. *Bonus to new partner.* Goodwill brought to the enterprise by the new partner is not recorded as an asset. The investment of the new partner is recorded by debiting assets with the amount invested, excluding goodwill, debiting the capital accounts of the old partners with the amount of the bonus, and crediting the new partner's capital account with the total.

5. *Neither goodwill nor bonus recognized.* The investment of the new partner is recorded by debiting assets and crediting his capital account with the amount of the investment.

PROPRIETARY ACCOUNTS

In the partnership two accounts are ordinarily kept for each partner. One is his Capital account and the other is his Personal, or Drawing, or Current, account.

The capital and personal accounts are maintained like those of the single proprietorship referred to above.

DISPOSITION OF PROFIT AND LOSS

The balance of the Profit and Loss Summary account is distributed to the partners in the ratio indicated by the copartnership agreement; or if no provision is made, profits and losses are shared equally among the partners. Each partner's share of the profit or loss may be closed to his Personal account or to his Capital account in a manner similar to that employed in the single proprietorship.

Bases for Distribution of Profit and Loss. Following are various ways in which the copartnership agreement may provide for the division of profits and losses:

1. Arbitrary, or fixed, ratio, including equal division

2. Investment ratio, including original investment, investment at certain dates, or average investment

3. Interest on investment and distribution of **remainder** on another basis

4. Salaries to partners and distribution of remainder on another basis

5. Any combination of the above bases.

DISSOLUTION

The dissolution of the partnership comes about when the copartnership agreement is terminated by an act of the parties, by automatic operation of the law, or by action of the courts.

Reasons for Partnership Dissolution. A partnership may be dissolved for the following reasons:

1. Accomplishment of the purpose for which the partnership was formed

2. Passage of a specific period of time, or occurrence of a specified event

3. Decision to become incorporated

4. Sale of the firm

5. Admission of a new partner

6. Retirement of a partner

7. Death of a partner

8. Bankruptcy of a partner

9. Failure of the firm

10. Illegality

11. Declaration of war between the country in which the partnership was formed, and a country in which one or more of the partners are citizens

12. Incapacity or insanity of a partner

13. Misconduct of a partner

14. Disagreement among the partners which cannot be settled, or unwillingness to continue the association

15. Inability to perform the work for which the partnership was formed.

Dissolution terminates a partnership, but it does not necessarily cause· the discontinuance of the business. The business may be continued by a different partnership or other form of business organization.

Distribution of Partnership Assets. In case of liquidation of a partnership, the assets are distributed in the following order:

1. Payment to creditors other than partners

2. Repayment by partners of loans or advances which do not constitute capital investment

3. Distribution to the partners of any profit or loss resulting from the liquidation

4. Return of the investment of the partners.

ADDITIONAL BIBLIOGRAPHY*

Bolon, Dallas S., *Introduction to Accounting,* 2nd ed. New York: John Wiley & Sons, Inc., 1938. Pp. 277-321.

Cole, Dana F., *Beginning Accounting.* New York: Thomas Y. Crowell Co., 1940.   Pp. 291-297, 593-628.

Elwell, Fayette H., *Elementary Accounting.* Boston: Ginn and Co., 1945. Pp. 10-16, 316-331, 624-642.

Hatfield, Henry R., Sanders, Thomas H., and Burton, Norman L., *Accounting Principles and Practices.* Boston: Ginn and Co., 1940. Pp. 219-240.

Howard, Stanley E., *The A B C of Accounting,* 3rd ed. Princeton: Princeton University Press, 1938. Pp. 249-257.

Jackson, J. Hugh, *Accounting Principles.* Los Angeles: Charles R. Hadley Co., 1944. Pp. 101-104, 639-668.

Kelley, Arthur C., *Essentials of Accounting.* New York: American Book Co., 1935. Pp. 7-8, 196-223.

* For other references, see the QUICK REFERENCE TABLE TO STANDARD TEXTBOOKS in the forepart of this book.

Kennedy, Donald D., Esterly, George R., and von Minden, William J., *Introductory Accounting*. New York: The Ronald Press Co., 1942. Pp. 75-76, 467-496.

Lamberton, Robert A., *Fundamentals of Accounting*. New York: Longmans, Green and Co., 1942. Pp. 229-275.

Prickett, Alva L., and Mikesell, R. Merrill, *Principles of Accounting*, rev. ed. New York: The Macmillan Co., 1937. Pp. 262-367.

Rorem, C. Rufus, and Kerrigan, Harry D., *Accounting Method*, 3rd ed. New York: McGraw-Hill Book Co., Inc., 1942. Pp. 245-255, 432-439.

Scovill, Hiram, T., and Moyer, C. A., *Fundamentals of Accounting*. Boston: D. C. Heath and Co., 1940. Pp. 562-584.

XI

Corporation

A corporation, as defined by Chief Justice Marshall in a famous decision in 1819, "is an artificial being, invisible, intangible, and existing only in contemplation of the law." A corporation is a distinct legal entity, separate from the individuals who own it. A large part of the growth of the corporate form of business enterprise has occurred since the middle of the nineteenth century. It is the dominant form of organization for large-scale enterprises. Some of the characteristics that distinguish a corporation from other forms of business organization are: separate legal individuality and existence, charter granted by the state, proprietorship interest shown by shares of stock which are transferable units of proprietorship, limited liability of stockholders, continuity of existence, limitation of action.

Advantages of the Corporation.

1. Limitation of the stockholder's liability to a fixed amount, usually the amount of his investment

2. Ownership readily transferable

3. Separate legal existence

4. Stability and relative permanence of existence

5. Ease of securing capital in large amounts and from many investors, through the issuance of various stocks and long-term bonds

6. Delegated authority. Centralized control secured when owners delegate authority to hired managers.

Disadvantages of the Corporation.

1. Activities limited by the charter
2. Manipulation—minority stockholders sometimes exploited
3. Extensive government regulation and burdensome local, state, and federal reports
4. Numerous and sometimes excessive taxes
5. Indirect reward when manager does not share in the profits.

FORMATION OF THE CORPORATION

A corporation usually is formed by the authority of some state government. Corporations which do business in more than one state must comply with the federal laws regarding interstate commerce, and with the state laws, which may vary considerably in each state in which they operate.

The procedure ordinarily required to form a corporation is, first, that subscriptions to capital stock must be taken and a tentative organization created, and, second, that approval must be obtained from the Secretary of State in the state in which the corporation is to be formed. This approval is in the form of a charter for the corporation stating the powers and limitations of the particular enterprise.

LEGAL PROBLEMS OF THE CORPORATION

The charter states the things which a corporation is permitted to do, and care should be taken to see that nothing is done which the corporation is not permitted to do. Corporations generally are subject to more legal restrictions and government regulation than are other forms of business enterprise.

A corporation, being a distinct legal entity, may sue and be sued in its own name.

ORGANIZATION EXPENSE

Costs incurred in the creation of a corporation represent capital expenditures. They are capitalized by being debited to an asset account, Organization Expense. Presumably, the value of this asset will last as long as the corporation exists, because any similar corporation would have to meet similar costs to become established. The value of a large organization expense item may be questioned by readers of the balance sheet, however, and it is considered conservative practice for many kinds of business to write off the account early in the life of the corporation, perhaps over a period of five years, as permitted by the 1954 Internal Revenue Code.

PROPRIETARY ACCOUNTS

In the single proprietorship and the partnership, each owner has at least one account representing his investment in the business. If he has another proprietorship account, such as a current Drawing account, it usually is closed into the permanent Capital account at the close of an accounting period, as indicated in Chapter X.

The proprietary accounts for a corporation consist principally of one Capital Stock account in the general ledger, unless there are several classes of stock, and of at least one surplus account. Details of the capital stock ownership are shown on the stubs of the capital stock certificates, and, in the larger enterprises, in separate capital stock ledgers which are subsidiary to the general ledger account.

Capital stock is the evidence of ownership of a corporation. It is divided into equal shares, which are represented by capital stock certificates held by the owners (known as *stockholders*) and recorded as a total in the Capital Stock account. If there are several classes of stock, the shares in each class are uniform, but they differ from the shares in other classes.

The Capital Stock account does not change with ordinary transfers of stock ownership from one holder to another, but may be changed when either the number of shares outstanding or the valuation placed on each share is changed.

Control of a corporation is vested in its stockholders, who exercise their control by vote. Some classes of stock do not carry the voting privilege, and are known as *non-voting stock*. Holders of *voting stock* may participate in stockholders' meetings, held annually or oftener. At these meetings stockholders receive reports on the operations of the enterprise, pass on important phases of its activities, and elect a small group from their number to represent them as *directors* in a somewhat more active and direct control of the business.

Stockholders may not withdraw profits from a corporation at will. They are entitled to their proportionate share only to the extent that dividends are declared by the directors.

CLASSES OF CAPITAL STOCK

There are two principal classes of capital stock, *common* and *preferred*. Many varieties exist within these classes, providing for different rights relating to income, control, and treatment in case of dissolution. If only one class of stock is issued, it is common stock, although it may be called simply *capital stock*.

COMMON STOCK

Common stock represents the ownership of stockholders who have a residual claim on the assets of the corporation after all other claims have been met.

There may be more than one class of common stock, such as classes *A* and *B*. These differ in such matters as amount of control exercised over the corporation, and share of the profits.

PREFERRED STOCK

Stock which has priority over other stock of the same company, either with respect to its share of profits or to its share of assets in case of dissolution, or both, is called preferred stock. Owners of preferred stock have the same rights as owners of common stock, in addition to the priority rights, unless otherwise specified. There is no guarantee, however, that dividends will be paid or that the investment itself will ultimately be repaid.

Cumulative Features. Stock which is preferred as to dividends is cumulative unless otherwise specified. All unpaid dividends on cumulative stock must be paid before earnings may be distributed to the holders of common stock. Preferred stock which indicates that it does not have the cumulative provision is *non-cumulative*. Preferred stock may be non-cumulative for a specified period of time and then become cumulative.

Participation. After provision has been made for dividends on preferred stock at the stated rate, the holders of such stock may be entitled to share with the holders of common stock in any remaining amount available for dividends. Such participation becomes effective in some instances after a specified amount has been distributed to the holders of common stock. If preferred stock participates in the earnings beyond the stated dividend rate, it is called *participating,* and if it is limited to the stated dividend rate, it is *non-participating*.

TYPES OF STOCK VALUE

Par Value. Par value of stock is a nominal figure given to shares of capital stock as stated in a corporation's charter and on its stock certificates. Par value has no necessary relation to the price of the stock. It may indicate the amount paid for the stock when originally issued, but stock can be issued originally at a price above par, or even below par when permitted by law.

Par value stock is capital stock which has a par value, usually $100 a share. It is customary to show this value in a Capital Stock account. *No-par stock* is capital stock to which no par value has been assigned. No-par stock, if it has no stated value, is recorded in a Capital Stock account at the issuing price or prices.

Book Value. Book value of stock is the value per share of capital stock based on proprietorship. When there is only one class of capital stock, book value is determined by dividing total proprietorship (total book value) by the number of shares outstanding. When there are several classes of capital stock, the portion of proprietorship assignable to any one class is the basis for determining the book value of that class.

Market Value. Market value of stock is the price per share at which the stock is currently selling in the market.

Stated Value. Stated value of stock is the valuation per share placed on no-par stock by the stockholders or the board of directors. When stock has a stated value, that is the amount properly shown in the Capital Stock account, and amounts in excess of stated value received from sales of the stock are credited to Paid-in Surplus.

RECORDING SALE OF STOCK

There are two commonly accepted methods of recording the sale of capital stock. The method chosen should be adopted at the time the formation of the corporation is recorded in the accounting records. It is desirable, regardless of the method used, to place at the beginning of the journal at least a brief description of the new corporation. Sometimes this description is rather extensive, including a copy of the charter and other documents required at the organization of the enterprise. Names of the accounts that record capital stock transactions vary somewhat at times, but the designations given below are widely approved.

If there are two or more classes of capital stock, separate accounts should be kept for them so that transactions relating to each class are clearly distinguishable. For instance, there should be separate accounts for Subscriptions Receivable, Common, and for Subscriptions Receivable, Preferred.

1. *Pro forma method.* When a bookkeeper employs this method, he makes the first journal entry relating to capital stock by debiting Unissued Capital Stock account and crediting Authorized Capital Stock with the entire amount of stock authorized by the charter.[1] This entry is sometimes called the *pro forma entry.*

In the next entry he debits Subscriptions Receivable and credits Capital Stock Subscribed with the amount of subscriptions to capital stock received. There may be one such entry, or many. If the subscribers agree to pay more or less than par for the stock, Subscriptions Receivable account is debited with the amounts to be received, Capital Stock Subscribed is credited with the par value of the stock to be issued, and the difference is credited to Premium on Stock if the price is above par, or debited to Discount on Stock if the price is below par.

Subscriptions Receivable constitute an asset of the firm. They represent legally enforceable contracts with purchasers of capital stock. The Capital Stock Subscribed account represents a liability of the firm to issue capital stock to the subscribers in accordance with their contracts.

In the third entry the bookkeeper debits Cash or other asset accounts, and credits Subscriptions Receivable with the amount received on the Subscriptions. In the fourth entry he debits Capital Stock Subscribed and credits Unissued Capital Stock with the amount of stock issued to subscribers.

This method has the merit of showing in the

---

1 The amount entered is the total par value or the total stated value of the stock. The pro forma method cannot be used for no-par stock which has no stated value, but when following an alternative method the number of shares authorized should be written as a memorandum in the Capital Stock account.

account balances the total amount of capital stock authorized by the corporation charter and the amount not yet issued.

2. *An alternative method.* The bookkeeper may begin his entries by debiting Subscriptions Receivable and crediting Capital Stock Subscribed with the amount of subscriptions received, treating premium or discount on the capital stock as described above. He then debits Cash, or other asset accounts, and credits Subscriptions Receivable with the amount received on the subscriptions. These entries are exactly like the second and third entries under the pro forma method. When stock is issued to the subscribers, the amount is debited to Capital Stock Subscribed and credited to Capital Stock.

PREMIUM AND DISCOUNT ON STOCK

Capital Stock may be issued for more or less than its par value. The amount received above par is a *premium,* which is credited to an account, Premium on Stock, or, if preferred, to Capital Surplus or Paid-in Surplus. Where state laws permit the issue of stock for less than par, the amount received below par is a *discount* which is debited to an account, Discount on Stock.

Premium on stock should appear in the net worth section of a balance sheet as an addition to the par value of stock outstanding. It represents capital in excess of par value invested by the owners.

Discount on stock should appear on the balance sheet as a deduction from the par value of stock outstanding. It is not an asset, but measures the amount below par invested by the stockholders. A concern, having sold stock at a discount, may desire to close out the discount account so that it will not appear as a separate item on the balance sheet.

This is accomplished by debiting Surplus and crediting Discount on Stock.

No-par stock which has a stated value may be issued for more than that value, and, if permitted by law, it may be issued for less than that value. The resulting premium or discount is handled like the premium or discount on par value stock. Instead of selling stock at less than stated value, however, it would be desirable to reduce the stated value.

RECORDS PECULIAR TO THE CORPORATION

In addition to the usual journals and ledgers kept by all types of business organizations, a corporation needs a minute book and stock certificates and may use other special records relating to its proprietary accounts. Some of these records are as follows:

1. *Minute book.* A record of the proceedings of the meetings of stockholders and of the board of directors

2. *Stock certificate book.* This book contains serially numbered blank stock certificates, to be issued to stockholders, and attached stubs, to be retained as a record of stock outstanding. When a certificate is canceled, the usual practice is to attach it to its stub.

3. *Stock subscription book.* A book containing the subscription blanks on which subscribers contract for purchases of capital stock

4. *Subscribers' cash receipts journal.* A special cash book which shows the amounts of payments on stock subscriptions

5. *Subscribers' ledger.* A subsidiary ledger which contains the individual subscribers' accounts and is controlled by the general ledger account, Subscriptions Receivable

6. *Stockholders' ledger, or capital stock ledger.* A record of the capital stock outstanding, which contains a separate account for each stockholder showing the number of shares he owns and his stock certificate serial numbers and dates

7. *Stock transfer journal.* A journal used to record the transfer of stock from one stockholder to another.

TREASURY STOCK

Treasury stock is capital stock which has been issued and paid for in full and later reacquired by the issuing corporation as a result of purchase or donation. Methods of accounting for treasury stock vary. The following are representative procedures.

Treasury stock with par value is debited to Treasury Stock account at par. If it is purchased at a premium, the amount of premium is debited to an account, Premium on Treasury Stock, or to Capital Surplus. If it is purchased at a discount, the amount of discount is credited to Discount on Treasury Stock, or to Capital Surplus. If treasury stock is purchased, Cash or some other asset account is credited, but if it is received as a gift, the par value is credited to Donated Surplus. If no-par stock is reacquired, it is entered in a Treasury Stock account either at cost or at the average selling price of the stock.

Accounts for premium and discount on treasury stock are closed into Capital Surplus at the end of the accounting period, or, in order to avoid a debit balance in Capital Surplus, they may be closed to Earned Surplus. Gains or losses on disposition of treasury stock may be transferred in the same manner to Capital Surplus or to Earned Surplus.

Treasury stock is treated by some corporations as an asset, a temporary investment held for resale. Another view, generally preferred, is that treasury stock represents a reduction of capital stock outstanding, and should be shown on the balance sheet as a deduction from the amount of stock issued.

DONATED STOCK

Donated stock is treasury stock which has been donated by stockholders. Usually the purpose is to permit the corporation to sell the stock for needed working capital.

The entry recording the gift debits Treasury Stock or Donated Stock, and credits Donated Surplus with the par value of the stock. Sales of the stock at less than par decrease the donated surplus, and sales at more than par increase it. Donated surplus is a capital surplus representing additional investment in the business, and should not be confused with the earned surplus.

WATERED STOCK

Watered stock is stock for which assets have been received in full payment at an inflated value. The amount of *water* in the stock is the excessive valuation placed on the assets.

SURPLUS

Surplus, as the term is ordinarily used in accounting, is the excess of proprietorship over the capital stock of a corporation. If proprietorship is less than the capital stock, a deficit exists. A surplus account which has a debit balance is generally called a *deficit* on the balance sheet, and should be shown as a deduction from proprietorship.

Surplus is generally divided into *capital surplus* and *earned surplus*. Capital surplus includes all additions to the net worth of a corporation which do not represent earnings properly credited to earned surplus, or additional capital stock properly credited to a capital stock account. Earned surplus consists of undistributed earnings of a corporation.

There is general agreement among accountants on the

broad definitions of surplus, but opinions differ on the exact classifications in borderline cases.

The principal classes of surplus should be shown separately on the balance sheet, and where it seems necessary for a clear interpretation of the figures the important subdivisions should be indicated separately. Classified according to source, surplus may be divided into three groups, as follows:

1. *Contributed surplus*. This is a capital surplus. On the balance sheet it frequently bears the title *capital surplus*. It results from transactions involving such items as: premium on sales of capital stock (often listed separately as *paid-in surplus*), assessments against stockholders, forfeitures of stock subscription deposits and rights, gifts of property or of the corporation's own stock (*donated surplus*), and profit on purchases and sales of treasury stock.

2. *Revaluation surplus*. This is a surplus which is credited when a fixed asset account is written up to reflect an increase in value over the amount previously shown. It is generally classified as a capital surplus and is listed separately on the balance sheet.[2]

3. *Earned surplus*. Earned surplus is an accumulation of undistributed earnings. It is the principal factor by means of which the net worth of a corporation is increased. There are two important subdivisions of earned surplus. They are: (1) *appropriated surplus*, which includes portions of surplus set aside in separate accounts for special purposes, such as a reserve for sinking fund, and (2) *unappropriated surplus*, which is available for dividends.[3]

---

2 A revaluation surplus may be given other titles, such as surplus arising from revaluation of assets, reappraisal surplus, unearned surplus, and surplus from appreciation of assets.

3 Appropriated surplus is also called restricted surplus. Usually it appears in several surplus reserve accounts. Unappropriated surplus appears under various titles, such as unrestricted surplus, free surplus, undivided profits, earned surplus, or surplus.

DISPOSITION OF PROFIT AND LOSS

A corporation's net profit or loss for an accounting period is transferred from the Profit and Loss account to Earned Surplus account when the books are closed. The present tendency is to include in the Profit and Loss account all items affecting profits; but some extraordinary gains or losses and corrections of profits of previous periods are transferred directly to Surplus without passing through the Profit and Loss account; and sometimes dividends and appropriations of surplus are debited to Profit and Loss, or Net Income account, before the balance is transferred to Surplus.

Accumulated profits in the Surplus account are reduced by (1) losses, (2) transfers to appropriated surplus accounts (surplus reserve accounts), and (3) dividends declared.

DIVIDENDS

A dividend is ordinarily a proportional distribution of earnings to the stockholders. It is not an expense. The directors alone have the right to declare dividends. A stockholder may claim a share of the profits only to the extent that dividends have been declared.

Payment of a cash dividend out of capital surplus is legal under some circumstances, but is usually to be avoided because it is, in effect, a return of capital, not profits. A stock dividend out of a capital surplus merely has the effect on the balance sheet of shifting the amount of the dividend from Capital Surplus to Capital Stock.

Dividends Out of Capital. If a dividend is paid in excess of the amount of surplus, the excess is actually a return of invested capital. It is unlawful, generally, to pay dividends out of capital except: (1) when a corporation goes out of business and distributes the proceeds from sales of its assets to creditors and stockholders as *liquidating dividends,* and (2) when an enterprise dealing in wasting assets, such as a mine or a timber tract, desires to distribute to its stockholders not only the profits made, but also portions of the invested capital recovered from sales of the product and not required for reinvestment by the company.

Any dividend which impairs capital should be clearly identified so that the recipients will know that they are receiving a return of part of their invested capital.

Dividends Out of Earnings. Dividends paid out of earnings can be classified conveniently into four groups, as follows:

1. *Cash dividends.* The great majority of dividends are paid in cash.

2. *Commodity dividends.* Occasionally this form of dividend, known also as a *dividend in kind,* is declared, payable in assets of the corporation other than cash.

3. *Scrip dividends.* Corporations facing a temporary shortage of cash sometimes issue dividends in scrip, or notes, payable at a future date. If dividends have been paid regularly, this method prevents a break in the continuity of the payments, called *passing* a dividend. Ordinarily, however, the practice of issuing scrip dividends is not advisable.

4. *Stock dividends.* A dividend need not require the reduction of net worth and the disposal of assets. It can be paid in stock of the corporation if there is unissued stock or treasury stock available. Usually a stock dividend is declared out of earned surplus, with the result that the amount of the dividend is transferred on the books of the corporation from surplus available for dividends to a capital stock account, without a change in the total net worth or the total assets. The accumulated earnings so transferred

become a part of the permanent invested capital of the enterprise.

Entries to Record Dividends. The declaration and payment of a dividend can be journalized in a simple manner, as follows:

(1)

Surplus	5,000.00	
Dividends Payable		5,000.00

To record declaration of 5% cash dividend, payable June 25, 19—, to stockholders of record June 15, 19—.

(2)

Dividends Payable	5,000.00	
Cash		5,000.00

To record payment of dividend.

The Dividends Payable account is a liability of the corporation. If a dividend is to be paid in property, scrip, or stock, instead of cash, the entry to record the declaration can be similar to the first entry above, with a distinctive title, such as Stock Dividend Payable, if desired, and the proper description. Payment of such a dividend will require an entry similar to the second entry above, with a credit to the proper account.

CAPITAL STOCK AND SURPLUS ON THE BALANCE SHEET

The various kinds of capital stock should be shown separately on the balance sheet. If there is any unissued stock or treasury stock, the amounts should ordinarily be disclosed in the net worth section of the balance sheet.

All corporation surplus accounts should appear in the net worth section also, grouped according to kinds. Then the sum of all capital stock and surplus items is the recorded net worth of the corporation.

ADDITIONAL BIBLIOGRAPHY*

Bolon, Dallas S., *Introduction to Accounting,* 2nd ed. New York: John Wiley & Sons, Inc., 1938. Pp. 322-369.

Cole, Dana F., *Beginning Accounting.* New York: Thomas Y. Crowell Co., 1940. Pp. 297-311, 526-592.

Elwell, Fayette H., *Elementary Accounting.* Boston: Ginn and Co., 1945. Pp. 16-23, 250-264, 380-410, 535-556.

Harold. Gilbert, *An Outline of Corporation Finance.* New York: Barnes & Noble, Inc., 1946. Pp. 25-37.

Hatfield, Henry R., Sanders, Thomas H., and Burton, Norman L., *Accounting Principles and Practices.* Boston: Ginn and Co., 1940. Pp. 241-293.

Howard, Stanley E., *The A B C of Accounting,* 3rd ed. Princeton: Princeton University Press, 1938. Pp. 257-261.

Jackson, J. Hugh, *Accounting Principles.* Los Angeles: Charles R. Hadley Co., 1944. Pp. 104-106, 424-463.

Kelley, Arthur C., *Essentials of Accounting.* New York: American Book Co., 1935. Pp. 224-268.

Kennedy, Donald D., Esterly, George R., and von Minden, William J., *Introductory Accounting.* New York: The Ronald Press Co., 1942. Pp. 71-74, 497-547.

Lamberton, Robert A., *Fundamentals of Accounting.* New York: Longmans, Green and Co., 1942. Pp. 276-345.

Prickett, Alva L., and Mikesell, R. Merrill, *Principles of Accounting,* rev. ed. New York: The Macmillan Co., 1937. Pp. 368-468.

Rorem, C. Rufus, *Accounting Method,* 2nd ed. Chicago: The University of Chicago Press, 1930. Pp. 249-267, 374-385.

Scovill, Hiram T., and Moyer, C. A., *Fundamentals of Accounting.* Boston: D. C. Heath and Co., 1940. Pp. 585-624.

---

* For other references, see the QUICK REFERENCE TABLE TO STANDARD TEXTBOOKS in the forepart of this book.

XII

Bonds—Funds—Reserves

BONDS AN EVIDENCE OF INDEBTEDNESS

A bond is a promise, under seal, to pay a specified sum of money at a definite future date, usually with interest at a specified rate payable periodically.

There is little significant difference between bonds and promissory notes. A bond is a more formal document than a note. It must be executed under seal, while a note need not be. The expression *under seal* means that a signature is accompanied by the word "seal" or by some other symbol. Under some laws, a contract under seal possesses greater force than an ordinary contract. A bond ordinarily matures after ten, twenty, or more years, while most notes are made for short terms. Both bondholders and the owners of a corporation's promissory notes are creditors of the issuing corporation, and not owners as are the stockholders.

A bond is a unit in a series of similar bonds. The face value (par value or principal) is commonly $1,000, but other denominations are not unusual. Interest paid on a bond is a fixed amount determined by the stated rate and the face value, regardless of the price at which the bond is sold.

TYPES OF BONDS

Bonds differ in their provisions in a bewildering variety of ways. These variations provide bases for many types of classification, five of which are given below, together with brief descriptions of various bonds. Any specific bond can be classified under each of the following types.

Purpose for which Bonds are Issued.

1. Adjustment bonds, issued to readjust the amount of debt

2. Consolidated bonds, issued to replace several bond issues and simplify the debt structure

3. Funding bonds, issued to consolidate unfunded debt, or debt represented by notes and accounts payable

4. Refunding bonds, issued to replace an existing funded debt, or debt represented by bonds

5. Purchase money bonds, issued in part or full payment for property purchased

6. Construction, extension, and improvement bonds, issued to obtain funds for purposes specified.

Nature of the Issuing Authority.

1. Governmental bonds, issued by federal and state governments and their instrumentalities

2. Commercial bonds, issued by railroads, public utilities, and financial and industrial enterprises.

Character of Security of Principal.

1. *Unsecured* bonds. These bonds have no assets pledged as security for their payment. They are merely general obligations of the issuing company. They are generally called debentures.

2. *Secured* bonds. These bonds have certain assets pledged as security for their payment. They may be classified as follows:

   a. Mortgage bonds, usually secured by a mortgage on real estate

   b. Collateral trust bonds, usually secured by a lien on bonds or other securities, or personal property

c. Equipment obligations, usually secured by a lien on the equipment for the purchase of which they were issued

d. Guaranteed bonds, for which the security is the guaranty of another company.

Manner of Interest Payment.

1. Registered bonds, each of which bears the owner's name, is non-negotiable, and provides that interest payments be made by check direct to the registered owner

2. Coupon bonds, each of which is payable to bearer, is negotiable, and is accompanied by coupons to be cashed on interest payment dates in lieu of direct interest payments from the issuing corporation

3. Registered coupon bonds, each of which bears the owner's name, is non-negotiable, and is accompanied by coupons payable to bearer for the interest payments.

Manner of Payment of Principal.

1. Gold, silver, and legal tender bonds, payable with the type of money specified

2. Serial bonds, providing for maturity of parts of the issue periodically

3. Straight bonds, providing for maturity of the entire issue at one time

4. Callable bonds, or redeemable bonds, subject to call for redemption by the issuing corporation prior to maturity

5. Sinking fund bonds, requiring the issuing corporation to set aside a sinking fund out of which to pay the bonds at maturity

6. Convertible bonds, permitting the exchange of the bonds for other securities of the issuing corporation at the option of the bondholders and according to the terms specified.

BOND PRICES

There are a number of factors which determine the price at which a bond is sold. One of the most important and most obvious factors is the security of the bond, which is measured by the prospect of regularity of interest payments and ultimate repayment of the principal. When bonds of equal security are compared, the most important factor in determining price is the interest rate.

The *nominal* interest rate is the rate stated in the bond. It is the rate at which interest payments are made, based on the face value of the bond, regardless of its selling price.[1] The *effective* interest rate is the rate of return based on the actual price at which the bond was transferred.[2] If a bond sells at par, the nominal and effective rates are the same.

Premium on Bonds. If the nominal rate on a bond is higher than the *market* rate of interest (the rate of return which investors in the open market are willing to accept at a given time on that type of investment), the bond will sell for more than face value, and the difference between the selling price and par is premium.

The premium on bonds payable is in effect a liability. Each interest payment will be at the coupon rate and will include in part interest cost and in part a return of a portion of the premium. The amount of premium received should ordinarily be written off, or amortized, over the life of the bonds.

Discount on Bonds. If the nominal rate on a bond is

---

1 The nominal interest rate is also known as the coupon rate and the stated rate.
2 The effective interest rate is also known as the yield rate and the effective yield.

lower than the market rate of interest, the bond will sell for less than face value, and the difference between the selling price and par is discount.

The discount on bonds payable is a deferred charge to interest expense. Sometimes it appears on the assets side on the balance sheet as a deferred charge. A preferable treatment is to show it as a valuation account offset against bonds payable. The amount of the discount should ordinarily be amortized over the life of the bonds.

It is seldom that the nominal rate and the effective rate of a bond are identical. This is due principally to fluctuations in the market rate of interest. The result is that most bonds are sold at either more or less than their face value.

A corporation might prefer to issue bonds with a nominal interest rate lower than the market rate, causing the bonds to sell at a discount, in order to make the interest cost seem lower than it would be if the same bonds bore a nominal rate higher than the market rate and sold at a premium. The nominal rate, however, does not control the actual interest cost, as determined by the effective rate, because proper accounting methods require that either a premium or a discount should be amortized in order to make the effective rate equal to the market rate at the time the bonds are sold.

DISPOSITION OF PREMIUM AND DISCOUNT ON BONDS

A bond generally requires payment of its face value at maturity, and any premium or discount associated with it should be written off by that time. The amount of premium or discount may be transferred to surplus in one sum when the bonds are sold, or when they are paid at maturity, but more accurate methods of accounting require that premium and discount be amortized over the life of the bonds to which they relate.

Amortization of bond premium or discount is the periodic writing down of the premium or accumulation of the discount over the life of the bonds. The balance remaining in a bond premium or discount account at any time is the *unamortized* balance. Frequently the titles Unamortized Premium on Bonds Payable and Unamortized Discount on Bonds Payable appear in the records.

Book value of a bond is the sum of the face value and the unamortized premium, or the difference between the face value and the unamortized discount.

If bonds are sold above face value the premium should appear on the credit side of a Premium on Bonds Payable account. Entries to amortize the premium are made periodically, preferably at the time of each interest payment. When such an entry is made, the amount to be written off, as determined by the amortization method adopted, may be debited to Premium on Bonds Payable account and credited to Interest Expense account. This entry reduces the unamortized bond premium, and at the same time reduces the interest cost from the total coupon amount to the approximate amount it should be as determined by the effective rate of the bonds.

If bonds are sold for less than face value, the discount should appear on the debit side of a Discount on Bonds Payable account. An entry to record amortization of the discount may debit Interest Expense account and credit Discount on Bonds Payable account with the amount to be written off. This reduces the unamortized discount, and increases the interest cost above the total coupon amount to the approximate figure indicated by the effective rate of the bonds.

Any variations in the procedures for amortizing premium or discount on bonds should achieve substantially the same effects. The amortization may be recorded with the interest payment in one compound journal entry, as described later in this chapter.

The disposition of premium or discount on bonds is illustrated in the following examples:

1. *Straight line amortization.* The simplest plan of amortization is to write off an equal amount of the premium or discount applicable to each bond at each interest payment date. This is called the *straight line method,* or the *bonds outstanding method.* It is easy to understand and simple to operate, and, therefore, is widely used. However, it is not as accurate as the interest method.

2. *Interest method of amortization.* The method which provides for systematic writing off of bond premium or discount and at the same time achieves the most accurate record of interest cost, is the *interest method.* Under this plan, an issuing corporation may compute the amount of interest cost on its bonds at any time by multiplying the book value of the bonds at that time by the effective rate applicable to them. The difference between the interest so computed and the nominal interest is the amount of premium or discount to be amortized. Interest cost changes at each interest payment date, because of changes in the book value of the bonds brought about by amortization.

    Present value of the bonds at each interest payment date may be computed by mathematical formulas, and the difference between the values at the beginning and end of an interest period is the amount of premium or discount to be amortized. This is a variation of the interest method and should produce the same results as the application of effective rate.

3. *Bond table method of amortization.* Bond tables are published which give the present value of bonds on their interest payment dates at various nominal interest rates and various effective interest rates. Bond tables facilitate the computation of amortization of premium or discount by providing the present value at interest payment dates and eliminating the need for

computations by mathematical formulas as indicated above.

4. *Premium or discount closed to surplus.* If the amount of premium or discount is relatively small, it may be closed to Surplus or some other appropriate proprietorship account. This procedure makes it unnecessary to compute the amount of periodic amortization. The amount of the discount or premium is merely debited or credited to Surplus, as the case may be. In addition, small amounts may be debited or credited to Surplus when such action would make the balance of the premium or discount the exact amount for use with bond tables. This procedure is theoretically undesirable but when the amounts involved are small, the resulting error is also small.

5. *Use of amortization schedules.* Amortization schedules may be prepared for each bond issue at the time the bonds are issued. These schedules should include information desired at each interest payment date, such as the amount of interest to be paid, the amount to be charged to the interest expense account, the amount of premium or discount to be amortized, and the unamortized balance of premium or discount. The computations for amortization of bond premium or discount over the life of the bonds can be made at the time the bonds are issued and entered in an amortization schedule by interest payment dates. At the time of interest payments it is not necessary to make any additional computations, but only to look up in the amortization schedule the information necessary for proper journal entries.

ACCOUNTING FOR BONDS

The following discussion deals with the records for bonds payable. Assuming cash transactions, a representative

method of making the entries is given, but numerous variations are found. No discussion of the records to be kept
by the holder of bonds is undertaken here, since the problems are somewhat similar, differing principally in the fact
that the bonds are a liability of the issuing corporation and
an asset of the bondholder.[3]

A journal entry to record the sale of bonds or the payment
of interest on them, is influenced by the amount received
for the bonds, whether face value or more or less than face
value.

Recording Sale of Bonds.

1. *Sale at par.* When bonds are sold for their face
    value, the journal entry to record the sale is a debit
    to Cash and a credit to Bonds Payable for the amount
    of the bonds.

2. *Sale at a premium.* When bonds are sold for more
    than their face value, the journal entry to record the
    sale is a debit to Cash for the total amount received,
    a credit to Bonds Payable for the face value of the
    bonds issued, and a credit to Premium on Bonds Pay-
    able for the difference, which is the amount of the
    premium received.

3. *Sale at a discount.* When bonds are sold for less than
    their face value, the journal entry to record the sale
    is a debit to Cash for the amount received, a debit to
    Discount on Bonds Payable for the difference between
    the amount received and the face value of the bonds
    issued, and a credit to Bonds Payable for the face
    value of the bonds issued.

---

3 Bonds maturing more than a year in the future constitute fixed liabilities of the
issuing corporation. The same bonds may be either current or fixed assets of the
bondholder, depending upon whether he intends to hold them as temporary investments or as permanent investments.

This discussion has omitted the *pro forma entry*, preferred by some accountants, by which Unissued Bonds Payable would be debited and Authorized Bonds Payable credited for the face value of the bonds to be issued. If the pro forma method were used, a sale of bonds would be credited to Unissued Bonds Payable to reduce that account.

Expenses relating to the issuance of bonds, such as printing and registration expenses and legal fees, are properly chargeable to a bond premium or discount account.

Recording Interest Payments.

1. *On bonds sold at par.* A journal entry to record the payment of interest on bonds sold at par consists of a debit to Interest Expense and a credit to Cash for the amount paid.

2. *On bonds sold at a premium.* When the payment of interest on bonds sold at a premium is journalized, a compound entry may be made consisting of a debit to Interest Expense for the difference between the amount paid and the portion of premium to be amortized at that time, a debit to Premium on Bonds Payable for the amount of amortization, and a credit to Cash for the amount paid, which is at the nominal interest rate.

3. *On bonds sold at a discount.* When the payment of interest on bonds sold at a discount is journalized, a compound entry may be made consisting of a debit to Interest Expense for the sum of the amount paid and the portion of discount to be amortized at that time, a credit to Discount on Bonds Payable for the amount of amortization, and a credit to Cash for the amount paid, which is at the nominal interest rate.

Recording Principal Payments. When a payment of the principal of bonds payable is made, the journal entry to record such payment is a debit to Bonds Payable and a credit to Cash. In some cases, the record of the last interest payment and the payment of the bonds may be combined. If this is done, a compound journal entry is used, which is merely the combination of the entry for the payment of the principal, the entry for the payment of interest, and the writing off of any remaining premium or discount.

Records. The issuing corporation should keep such records as would be necessitated by the nature of the bond issue. If the bond issue is composed of coupon bonds, there is no need, ordinarily, for special records beyond the files of correspondence and contracts and the customary entries in journals and the general ledger. If, however, registered bonds are sold, either a bonds payable register, or a bonds payable subsidiary ledger, or both, must be maintained, in order to have a record of the bondholders.

FUNDS

The meanings of the words *funds* and *reserves* are frequently confused. These two terms are not synonymous .and care should be taken so that each is used correctly.

A *fund* is an asset, usually consisting of cash, securities, or both, set aside for a specific purpose. A fund account is an asset account representing cash, securities, or other assets set aside for a special purpose. The principal purpose for which a fund is originally established and periodically maintained is to have on hand particular assets with which to meet a future need which is definite and known in advance.

CLASSES OF FUNDS

The more important classes of funds established by business enterprises are as follows:

1. Funds for the acquisition of fixed assets. One type is the Plant Extension Fund, which is used in conjunction with the Reserve for Plant Extension account. In this way the management is assured that in accord-

ance with a definite plan assets will be set aside to pay for the expansion of the plant.

2. The *petty cash,* or *imprest,* fund, as previously explained, consists of cash set aside to take care of small miscellaneous expenditures which can be made most readily in cash.

3. *Branch* funds usually consist of cash sent to branches to facilitate their operation.

4. *Bond sinking* funds are used for the redemption of fixed liabilities. They may be created in accordance with the contract which exists between the enterprise and long-term creditors. They consist of cash or other assets which will be utilized to liquidate the obligation. The funds will be held by an impartial trustee if so required by the bond contract.

5. Miscellaneous funds may be established for various specific purposes, depending upon the needs of a particular enterprise.

RESERVES

The word *reserve* is frequently used in account titles. Much confusion has resulted from the wide variety of uses and meanings of the word. Reserve accounts ordinarily have credit balances. There are three varieties of reserve accounts: valuation, liability, and surplus.

Valuation Reserves. A valuation reserve is an account which exhibits the actual or estimated decrease in value shown in an asset account. This type of reserve, often called an allowance, is used when it is desired to retain the original, or historical, cost in the asset account. A valuation reserve is a contra, or offset, account. Examples are:

1. Reserve for Bad Debts
2. Reserve for Depreciation
3. Reserve for Depletion.

Liability Reserves. A liability reserve is an account which exhibits the actual or estimated amount of an accrued liability. Such a reserve might be more properly termed an *accrued liability.* Examples of liability reserve accounts are:

1. Reserve for Compensation Insurance

2. Reserve for Taxes.

Surplus Reserves. A surplus reserve is an account which exhibits the part of surplus set aside, or appropriated, for a particular purpose. This type of reserve is used when it is desired to decrease the amount available for dividends and, for the present, to retain within the enterprise the earnings so segregated. Surplus reserves are known also as proprietorship reserves and appropriated surplus reserves. Examples are:

1. Reserve for Contingencies

2. Reserve for Plant Extension

3. Reserve for Sinking Fund.

The terms *secret reserves* and *hidden reserves* are frequently used but do not refer to a specific reserve account. They refer rather to the understatement of proprietorship. This understatement is accomplished by undervaluing or omitting an asset or overvaluing a liability. The presence of a secret reserve causes erroneous values to be shown on the financial statements and conceals from stockholders and other interested persons the full value of the proprietorship.

Reserves and *funds* are accounting terms which, as previously stated, are frequently confused. The term reserve is sometimes used incorrectly to refer to a fund consisting of assets set aside for some particular purpose. A reserve and a fund may be used at the same time or they may be used separately. A reserve may be maintained even though no fund is provided, or a fund may be maintained even though no reserve is set up.

ACCOUNTING FOR RESERVES

Journal Record. When a reserve is established or increased, a journal entry is made to credit the proper reserve account. For a valuation reserve the corresponding debit is to an appropriate expense account. For a liability reserve the debit is usually to an expense account, but occasionally to Surplus or Earned Surplus Unappropriated. For a surplus reserve the debit is to Surplus or Earned Surplus Unappropriated.

Balance Sheet Presentation. A valuation reserve should appear on the balance sheet as a deduction from the asset which it values. The difference is the present estimated net value of such asset. Liability reserves are in reality a part of the liabilities. They should be shown on the balance sheet in the current liabilities section. Surplus reserves should be shown as part of surplus in the net worth section on the balance sheet.

ACCOUNTING FOR FUNDS

The entry to establish or increase a fund may be made by debiting the fund account and crediting Cash. When a fund is established for the purpose of acquiring fixed assets, an entry may be made at the same time to establish or increase a surplus reserve by debiting Earned Surplus Unappropriated and crediting a reserve account such as Reserve for Plant Extension.

If a fund is to be increased by interest earned by the assets in the fund, such increase is recorded by debiting the fund account and crediting an appropriate income account.

When the assets held in the fund are converted into the assets for which the fund was established, the net result in the records will be a debit to an account for the new assets and a credit to the fund account. At the time the fund account is closed, any surplus reserve account maintained in connection with it should be closed by a debit to the reserve account and a credit to Earned Surplus Unappropriated.

A sinking fund for the retirement of bonds, and other special funds, as well as any reserves established in connection with them, require somewhat similar bookkeeping procedures.

Funds should be shown on the balance sheet in a special classification between the current and the fixed groups, in the opinion of some authorities.[4]

ADDITIONAL BIBLIOGRAPHY*

Bolon, Dallas S., *Introduction to Accounting*, 2nd ed. New York: John Wiley & Sons, Inc., 1938. Pp. 211-220, 436-442.

Cole, Dana F., *Beginning Accounting*. New York: Thomas Y. Crowell Co., 1940. Pp. 523-532, 692-709, 750-756.

Elwell, Fayette H., *Elementary Accounting*. Boston: Ginn and Co., 1945. Pp. 467-489, 549-551.

Hatfield, Henry R., Sanders, Thomas H., and Burton, Norman L., *Accounting Principles and Practices*. Boston: Ginn and Co., 1940. Pp. 269-276, 282-286, 291-293

Howard, Stanley E., *The A B C of Accounting*, 3rd ed. Princeton: Princeton University Press, 1938. Pp. 147-183, 221-248.

Jackson, J. Hugh, *Accounting Principles*. Los Angeles: Charles R. Hadley Co., 1944. Pp. 464-480.

Kelley, Arthur C., *Essentials of Accounting*. New York: American Book Co., 1935. Pp. 259-260, 267-274.

Kennedy, Donald D., Esterly, George R., and von Minden, William J., *Introductory Accounting*, New York: The Ronald Press Co., 1942. Pp. 548-569.

Lamberton, Robert A., *Fundamentals of Accounting*. New York: Longmans, Green and Co., 1942. Pp. 315-324.

Rorem, C. Rufus, and Kerrigan, Harry D., *Accounting Method*, 3rd ed. New York: McGraw-Hill Book Co., Inc., 1942. Pp. 278-300.

Scovill, Hiram T., and Moyer, C. A., *Fundamentals of Accounting*. Boston: D. C. Heath and Co., 1940. Pp. 616-618.

---

4 Some authorities feel that a bond sinking fund should be shown as a fixed asset, as it is an investment to be held until the maturity of a long-term liability. Other authorities would show a bond sinking fund in the fixed liabilities section as a deduction from the fixed liability which it will liquidate.

* For other references, see the QUICK REFERENCE TABLE TO STANDARD TEXTBOOKS in the forepart of this book.

XIII

Industrial Accounting

A clear distinction can be made between a merchandising concern and a manufacturing enterprise. A merchandising enterprise purchases commodities and sells them in essentially the same form they had when acquired. A manufacturing enterprise, however, acquires commodities and applies labor to them, usually through the use of machinery, and produces a different commodity. This process creates many accounting problems, some of which are discussed in this chapter.

PRODUCTION PROBLEMS

Large-scale Production. Many manufacturing operations can be performed most effectively when they are conducted on a large scale. The very magnitude of such operations produces problems, many of which are of minor consequence in a small concern, and some of which are unknown to any but the largest concerns.

Some of these problems relate to the securing and proper training of personnel, the inability of managers to know all of the employees personally, the difficulty of obtaining competent superintendence, providing necessary capital, finding an adequate supply of raw material, and planning a smooth flow of the product through the plant in the manufacturing process.

Industrial Combinations. Additional problems arise from the fact that many manufacturing concerns have been formed by combinations, and that production methods have been changed as a result of the combinations. Some of these problems are: record keeping for diversified properties, especially depreciation; the flow of goods to the various plants, between the various plants, and from plants; personnel problems; and taxation.

Variety of Products. Frequently one industrial concern manufactures a number of different products. This fact is important in all phases of accounting, especially in cost accounting. The task of the cost accountant would be relatively simple in an enterprise which manufactures only one product and has only one plant. As the number of products is increased, the task of the cost accountant is complicated, and there is an increasing need for his services.

ELEMENTS OF MANUFACTURING COSTS

The three elements which enter the cost of manufacturing any product are raw materials, direct labor, and manufacturing expense, burden, or overhead. The sum of raw materials cost and direct labor cost may be called *prime cost,* prime cost plus overhead may be called *factory cost,* factory cost plus selling expenses equals *total cost,* and total cost plus profit or minus loss equals *selling price.*

ACCOUNTS IN A MANUFACTURING ENTERPRISE

In addition to many of the usual accounts found in mercantile and other enterprises, a typical manufacturing concern requires some accounts which are peculiar to its type of activities.

There are so many variations in the bookkeeping procedures of manufacturers, especially in relation to manufacturing costs, that only a general discussion of some typical procedures and accounts in a manufacturing enterprise is undertaken here.

1. *Inventories.* In a manufacturing business there are three inventories, raw materials, goods in process, and finished goods, which take the place of merchandise inventory in a mercantile concern. All three of these inventories may be taken by physical count, and, in addition, the raw materials and finished goods inventories may be maintained by perpetual inventory. A perpetual inventory is usually kept with a card for each item, on which all additions are entered in one set of columns and all withdrawals entered in another set of columns. The difference between additions and withdrawals can be entered in a third, or balance, set of columns. The sets of columns may include both quantity and price data, if desired.

2. *Purchases.* All purchases of raw materials are debited to a Raw Materials Purchases account. At the close of the fiscal period the balance of this account is closed into the Raw Materials Used account.

3. *Purchase Returns.* The Raw Materials Purchase Returns and Allowances account is credited for all returns and allowances in a manner similar to that used for the Purchase Returns and Allowances account in a mercantile enterprise. The account may be divided so as to separate returns from allowances. Purchase discounts may be shown in a separate account or in the account with returns and allowances. At the close of the fiscal period the balance of this account, or accounts, will be closed to the Raw Materials Used account.

4. *Labor.* Wages paid for direct labor and for indirect labor will be recorded in separate accounts. Direct Labor will be charged for all labor applied directly to the products, while Indirect Labor will be charged for such things as supervision, maintenance, and fac-

tory clerical work which cannot be allocated directly to the product. The Direct Labor account is closed into the Cost of Goods Manufactured account. The Indirect Labor account may be closed into the Overhead account, or Burden account.

5. *Factory Overhead.* In addition to indirect labor, the Overhead, or Burden, account may include such items as rent, heat, light, power, insurance, depreciation, and factory supplies. The Burden account is closed into the Cost of Goods Manufactured account. In a cost accounting system the burden may be distributed to the finished product upon the basis of direct labor, direct materials, machine hours, or some other appropriate method. When this is done, less than the total of the burden may be charged to the product, in which case the balance of the Burden account will be underabsorbed burden. More than the total of the burden may be charged to the product, in which case the credit balance of the Burden account will be overabsorbed burden.

6. *Manufacturing Cost of Goods Sold.* The Manufacturing Cost of Goods Sold account may be used to serve the same purpose as the Cost of Goods Sold account in a mercantile enterprise. The Manufacturing Cost of Goods Sold account is a summarizing account which is debited with the beginning inventory of goods in process, and the balance of the Cost of Raw Materials Used account, the Direct Labor account, and, sometimes, the Burden account. It is credited with the final inventory of goods in process. The balance may be closed to the Cost of Goods Sold account or the Profit and Loss Summary account.[1]

---

1 Some accountants prefer the use of additional summarizing accounts, such as Cost of Goods Manufactured and Manufacturing Summary. Other accountants would limit the number of summarizing accounts to one Profit and Loss account, where feasible.

7. *Plant Accounts.* An account may be maintained for
    each individual fixed asset. Frequently such detailed
    records are kept in a separate subsidiary ledger called
    the plant ledger. Special forms of ledger sheets are
    available which provide supplementary information
    regarding the individual fixed asset, such as: date of
    acquisition, cost, estimated life, depreciation rate,
    disposal, selling price or scrap price, and spaces for
    periodic depreciation charges.

8. *Intangibles.* Frequently a manufacturing enterprise
    will have accounts for such intangibles as goodwill,
    patents, trade-marks, copyrights, franchises, formu-
    las, leaseholds, and occasionally organization expense.
    The problem of placing an acceptable valuation upon
    such assets is sometimes difficult, although the gen-
    eral accounting rule is that if they are to be recog-
    nized as assets, they should be carried at cost less
    provision for the amount of decrease in value since
    date of acquisition.

9. *Factory Ledger Account.* It may be desirable to have
    more detailed accounts relating to manufacturing costs
    in an auxiliary, or subsidiary, self-balancing ledger
    termed the factory ledger. In this case, a controlling
    account, the Factory Ledger account, would be in-
    cluded in the general ledger. In the factory ledger,
    a General Ledger account would be placed. The Fac-
    tory Ledger account and the General Ledger account
    are known as interlocking, or reciprocal, accounts.
    They enable the factory ledger to be a self-balancing
    ledger. If an entry is contained partially in the fac-
    tory ledger, and the rest of the entry is contained
    in the general ledger, both of the reciprocal accounts
    will be used in making the complete entry. Some
    of the manufacturing accounts listed above might
    be included in such a factory ledger, and might

in turn be controlling accounts for other subsidiary ledgers.

STATEMENTS OF A MANUFACTURING BUSINESS

A work sheet is used extensively in preparation of financial statements of a manufacturing enterprise. Such a work sheet generally differs only slightly from that of a mercantile concern, the chief differences being that the work sheet of the manufacturing concern is likely to contain more accounts and to have an additional pair of columns for the manufacturing costs or cost of goods manufactured. This entails no change in the principles involved in the use of the work sheet, but merely an extension of the principles already discussed.

Financial Statements. A profit and loss statement for a manufacturing concern differs from the profit and loss statements previously discussed, not so much in the principal headings as in the detailed information included. Although no change need be made in the section headings, a section may contain either a greater number of items, or few, if any, while the details appear in a supplementary schedule. For instance, the cost of goods sold section for a manufacturing concern contains much more information and more numerous accounts than does the cost of goods sold section of a mercantile enterprise. Included in this are such things as additional inventories and manufacturing expenses, mentioned above. If this detailed information is not desired in the profit and loss statement, portions of it may be removed from the profit and loss statement and shown in supplementary schedules. Schedules supporting the cost of goods sold section may be prepared to include the manufacturing cost of goods sold, cost of goods manufactured, or merely manufacturing expenses. Other sections of the profit and loss statement may also give rise to supplementary schedules. Additional examples would be supplementary schedules for selling expenses, general expenses, and non-operating incomes and expenses.

Financial statements frequently appear in condensed form. They vary in the amount of detailed information shown as the purpose varies for which the statements are prepared. For instance, a statement for the use of the general public will probably be in the briefest possible form, statements prepared for the owners or stockholders will contain greater detail, and the statements prepared for the use of the managers will contain the greatest possible detail.

Comparative statements are frequently employed so that a statement for one fiscal period may be compared with the financial statements of one or more other fiscal periods. Comparative statements may be made up of any type of financial statement or schedule, and may be prepared with or without comparative percentages, or ratios.

The balance sheet for a manufacturing enterprise differs from the balance sheet for a mercantile enterprise particularly in the predominance of fixed assets and the greater number of intangibles. The arrangement of items on the balance sheet may be the same, although some manufacturing concerns prefer that the fixed assets be placed first, followed by the current assets, because of this predominance. If this arrangement is followed for the assets, a similar arrangement should be followed for the liabilities. This is in contrast to the current-to-fixed arrangement commonly employed and previously discussed.

Supplementary Schedules. When detailed information is not desired on the financial statements, supplementary schedules may be employed as suggested above, to show the details not desired on the financial statements themselves. This is true of both the profit and loss statement and the balance sheet.

Balance sheet schedules are frequently prepared for the following items: accounts receivable, accounts payable, investments, and fixed assets.

It may be desirable to show on the profit and loss statement the complete manufacturing cost of goods sold section, or it may be desirable to prepare a separate schedule of manufacturing expenses. If even less detail is desired on the profit and loss statement, a supplementary schedule may be prepared for the cost of goods manufactured. This schedule will include not only the manufacturing expenses, but also the beginning and closing inventories of both raw materials and goods in process, together with purchases, purchase returns and allowances, freight in, and direct labor. This schedule may be expanded into the manufacturing cost of goods sold schedule by the inclusion of both opening and closing inventories of finished goods.

Sundry Reports. In addition to the financial statements and supplementary schedules, additional reports may be employed by manufacturing enterprises. Most of these reports are used but little by persons other than the managers. Nevertheless, these reports are very valuable to them. Some examples of this type of report are the pay roll reports, tax reports, production reports, receiving reports, shipping reports, and inventories.

COST ACCOUNTING

Cost accounting, as defined in Chapter I, is the determination of costs of doing business, especially unit costs of production and distribution.

Whereas the methods of accounting discussed in previous chapters have endeavored to compute costs for a unit of time, the fiscal period, cost accounting endeavors to make computations on the basis of units of production or distribution. Cost accounting is relatively simple for an enterprise which produces only one product, for in this case costs may be computed in terms of units of production merely by dividing total costs for the period by the number of units produced during that period. In a manufacturing enterprise in which more than one item is produced, the problems of cost accounting are more difficult. In such case, cost accounting endeavors to allocate to each individual product its share of the costs. Costs so computed may provide a basis for determining the proper selling price and the gross profit on the sale of each item. Cost accounting also provides information to assist in the control of manufacturing operations.

There are many methods of cost accounting which are commonly employed in industry at the present time. Probably no one cost accounting system could be universally adopted, as the problems differ greatly among manufacturing enterprises.

Cost accounting is a specialized subject and is considered by many accountants to be a distinct field, separated from work of the general accountant.

ADDITIONAL BIBLIOGRAPHY*

Cole, Dana F., *Beginning Accounting*. New York: Thomas Y. Crowell Co., 1940. Pp. 429-443.

Elwell, Fayette H., *Elementary Accounting*. Boston: Ginn and Co., 1945. Pp. 440-463.

Hatfield, Henry R., Sanders, Thomas H., and Burton, Norman L., *Accounting Principles and Practices*. Boston: Ginn and Co., 1940. Pp. 297-303.

Howard, Stanley E., *The A B C of Accounting*, 3rd ed. Princeton: Princeton University Press, 1938. Pp. 184-197.

Kennedy, Donald D., Esterly, George R., and von Minden, William J., *Introductory Accounting*. New York: The Ronald Press Co., 1942. Pp. 570-601.

Lamberton, Robert A., *Fundamentals of Accounting*. New York: Longmans, Green and Co., 1942. Pp. 372-389.

Rorem, C. Rufus, *Accounting Method*, 2nd ed. Chicago: The University of Chicago Press, 1930. Pp. 268-277.

Scovill, Hiram T., and Moyer, C. A., *Fundamentals of Accounting*. Boston: D. C. Heath and Co., 1940. Pp. 5-9.

---

* For other references, see the QUICK REFERENCE TABLE TO STANDARD TEXTBOOKS in the forepart of this book.

XIV

Accounting for Departments, Branches, and Subsidiaries

DEPARTMENTS

A business enterprise generally sells more than one type of goods and services. In such cases it is desirable, though not always feasible, to compute the incomes and expenses and the resulting profit separately for each commodity or service. The method of accounting which provides such separation is known as *departmental accounting*. Departmentalized accounting does not ordinarily involve a separation of the balance sheet items by departments, but includes a separation into departments of some of the profit and loss statement items. The operating incomes will be separated by departments and a number of the expenses will be allocated to the proper departments. This does not provide a complete profit and loss statement for each department, since some income and expense items cannot readily be broken down by departments and are therefore shown under general headings on the profit and loss statement.

Accounts for Departments. Ordinarily, no entirely new accounts will be found to be necessary for departmentalized accounting. However, items of income and expense which are allocated to the departments will necessitate the subdivision of the accounts by departments. For instance, there will be a Sales account for each department which makes sales. Such an account will have the general title of the account, followed by the departmental designation. For example, the Sales accounts might be labeled *Sales - Department A, Sales - Department B,* etc.

Departmentalized Journals. The original record of transactions in departmentalized accounting should provide a method by which each transaction will be allocated to departments at the time it is recorded. In order that this may be done, each income and expense item which would ordinarily be given a special column in a journal, may instead be given as many columns as there are departmental accounts for that item. The column headings should include the proper departmental designations, such as those suggested above for account titles. For instance, the purchases journal will need only one column for accounts payable, as this is a balance sheet item, but it will need as many columns for purchases as there are departments for which purchases are made. The same situation may readily be true of all other special journals.

Adjustments. Some transactions may not be segregated by departments conveniently or accurately at the time they are recorded. Such transactions will be recorded originally as if no departments existed. At the close of the fiscal period, if not before, it will be necessary to make the proper allocation of such income and expenses as subsequent information would indicate to be desirable.

Financial Statements for a Departmentalized Enterprise. Ordinarily, no distinction as to departments will be made on the balance sheet. However, it is usually considered desirable to segregate the departmental profit and loss items, where convenient. In all cases it should be possible to obtain the gross profit for each department, as well as the total gross profit for the enterprise. In some enterprises it is not considered feasible to compute the net profit for each department. In fact, it may be that such computation cannot be made accurately. In other enterprises a net profit is computed for each department even if it necessitates the use of more or less arbitrary allocations. In all cases as much information as possible should be shown for each department, so that it may be known which departments are making profits, and which departments are operating at a loss. This information is important for management as an aid in formulating its policies.

BRANCHES

One phenomenon of the growth of business enterprises is the establishment of branches through which additional sales may be made. An example is the growth of the chain store, which has received much attention in recent years.

Care should be taken that the term *agency* is not confused with the term *branch*.

One type of agency consists merely of a sales office which does not carry a full stock of merchandise but takes orders which are delivered from the principal office, or home office. The customer is invoiced by the home office, which office also determines the credit to be extended and makes the collections.

Some offices, though not carrying a stock of merchandise, may invoice the customer, extend credit, and make the collections. Such an office has some of the characteristics of both an agency and a branch.

A branch usually maintains a sufficient inventory of merchandise to make deliveries to customers. All of this merchandise may be received from the general office, or part of it may be purchased from independent vendors. A branch maintains its own credit department and makes the collections. Many variations are possible, and the accounting provisions may differ in each type of branch or agency. Also, the accounting methods employed when there are a great many branches may differ from the accounting methods employed when there are only a few branches. The general principles involved are illustrated by the following discussion of a typical mercantile concern, assuming the existence of only a few branches.

Branch Accounting. The branch maintains a complete set of accounting records similar to those which would be used if the store were an independent enterprise. The principal distinction is that instead of proprietorship accounts, such as have been previously discussed, a Home Office account is used. This account represents the investment of the general, or central, office in the branch. The Home Office account in the branch ledger is reciprocal to the Branch Ledger account in the general ledger of the home office. The use of this reciprocal account makes the branch ledger a self-balancing ledger.

Use of Reciprocal Accounts. The controlling account, Branch Ledger, in the general ledger, is debited for the assets sent to the branch and for profit reported by the branch. It is credited for assets received from the branch and for losses reported by the branch. The reciprocal account, Home Office, in the branch ledger, is debited for assets sent to the home office and for losses incurred. It is credited for assets received from the home office and for profits. Since each of these accounts exhibits the same information, but on opposite sides, they are ordinarily termed *reciprocal or interlocking* accounts.

In addition to the set of accounting books provided for each branch, special records often are maintained in the home office. For instance, special books may be kept by the home office to record activities performed for the branches and not shown on the branch books in detail. Such activities may be recorded in summarized form on the branch books when periodic reports are received from the home office.

Financial Statements for an Enterprise with Branches.
Independent financial statements sometimes are prepared for
each branch and for the home office. An individual work
sheet can be used as an accounting tool in the preparation
of each of these statements, which is similar to the work
sheet previously discussed. In addition, the home office may
prepare a special combining work sheet from its books and
branch reports. In the use of this work sheet care should
be taken to provide for the elimination of intra-company
transactions. From such special work sheet the formal combined profit and loss statement and balance sheet will be
prepared.

In addition to the financial statements, various operating
reports may be prepared by each branch and by the home
office. These reports are prepared particularly for the use
of the management, according to its individual needs. Therefore, the extent, scope, and form of these reports will vary
greatly between enterprises.

TRENDS TOWARD BUSINESS COMBINATION

One phenomenon of the business world that has been
previously mentioned is the growth of large-scale business
enterprises. Large-scale enterprises frequently arise from
the combination of previously existing business units. Such
combinations are effected by mergers, consolidations, and
the creation of holding companies.

TYPES OF BUSINESS COMBINATIONS

Merger. A merger is a business combination in which
the acquiring company retains its name whereas the acquired
companies lose their identities. Such a merger means that
the purchasing company acquires the assets of the other
enterprises and assumes their liabilities. Payment for the
acquired companies may be made in any form, including
cash, or other assets, or stock in the purchasing corporation.

Consolidation. A consolidation is a business combination in which a new corporation is created which acquires the assets and assumes the liabilities of two or more previously existing companies. In a consolidation all the combined companies lose their identities. Payment for the acquired companies may be made in cash, or other assets, or in stock of the new corporation.

Holding Company. A *holding company* is a corporation whose principal function is to own at least a controlling amount of the capital stock outstanding of one or more other corporations, known as subsidiaries. A *parent company* differs from a holding company only in the fact that it is an operating company. The distinction is not always easily made, however, since some holding companies engage in operations in one or two departments. When more than 50 per cent of the outstanding capital stock is owned by another corporation, it should be obvious that a sufficient amount of stock is owned to control the subsidiary corporation. Quite frequently, much less than 50 per cent of the stock will be a sufficient amount to secure control. This is due to such factors as the wide spread of stock ownership, the antipathy of small stockholders to voting, the lack of organization of minority stockholders, and the willingness of small stockholders to vote with an organized group.

No difficulty of an unusual nature is encountered in preparing the financial statements for corporations combined through either a merger or a consolidation. In such cases there need be only one set of books, and the methods of preparing financial statements previously discussed may be readily employed. However, when a combination has been brought about through the holding company device, the preparation of useful financial statements is more difficult. For instance, both the holding company and the subsidiary companies retain their separate legal existences, yet the companies may be so interrelated that they comprise one financial entity. In the preparation of informative reports for a holding company, its financial statements must be combined with the financial statements of the subsidiary companies. Such a combination results in a consolidated balance sheet and a consolidated profit and loss statement.

CONSOLIDATED STATEMENTS

Consolidated financial statements are prepared by summarizing the statements of the affiliated companies and then eliminating intercompany transactions. It is fairly obvious that the balance sheets should be for the same date and that the profit and loss statements should include operations for the same period of time.

The Investment Account. A holding company's investment account is replaced on the consolidated balance sheet by the assets and liabilities of the subsidiary companies. Some holding companies operate on a limited scale, but in any case the investment account of a holding company does not provide a meaningful figure when it includes stock of subsidiary corporations. In the preparation of consolidated statements, a special work sheet is customarily, but not necessarily, used.

Intercompany Eliminations. Such eliminations are essential to the preparation of consolidated statements. They may be made in eliminations columns in the work sheet of the parent concern or holding company. Four principal groups of intercompany eliminations are as follows:

1. *Intercompany receivables and payables.* Advances, accounts receivable, notes receivable, and bonds are included in these eliminations when they are a part of transactions between affiliated companies.

2. *Intercompany profits in inventories.* These should not be shown on the financial statements. Profits should be eliminated which arise from intercompany trans-

actions involving merchandise still on hand at the close of the fiscal period.

3. *Investments in subsidiaries.* Such investments should not be shown on the consolidated balance sheet, although investments in corporations may be included if they are not sufficiently large to bring about control.

4. *Intercompany profit and loss items,* including sales and purchases and intercompany dividends, should be eliminated from the consolidated profit and loss statement since they are transactions between parts of a financial entity.

Periodic Financial Statements. A consolidated profit and loss statement and balance sheet are prepared as if the affiliated companies were a single unit. If the holding company owns 100 per cent of the outstanding capital stock of the subsidiary companies, the preparation of the financial statements is relatively easy. Frequently, however, the amount of stock owned is less than 100 per cent, making the procedure for preparation of the financial statement more complicated if an accurate and true picture of the affiliated group is to be shown. Particularly important is the showing of the status of minority stockholders within the group. Usually, the holdings of minority stockholders are shown as a part of net worth on the consolidated balance sheet, but sometimes they are listed as liabilities.

ADDITIONAL BIBLIOGRAPHY*

Accountants' Handbook, 4th ed. New York: The Ronald Press Co., 1957. Pp. 2:54, 5:41-47, 23:1-70.

Cole, Dana F., *Beginning Accounting.* New York: Thomas Y. Crowell Co., 1940. Pp. 398-428.

Elwell, Fayette H., *Elementary Accounting.* Boston: Ginn and Co., 1945. Pp. 348-368.

Hatfield, Henry R., Sanders, Thomas H., and Burton, Norman L., *Accounting Principles and Practices.* Boston: Ginn and Co. 1940. Pp. 179, 399-422.

---

* For other references, see the QUICK REFERENCE TABLE TO STANDARD TEXTBOOKS in the forepart of this book.

Jackson, J. Hugh, *Accounting Principles.* Los Angeles: Charles R. Hadley Co., 1944. Pp. 391-423, 580-584, 669-688.

Lamberton, Robert A., *Fundamentals of Accounting.* New York: Longmans, Green and Co., 1942. Pp. 346-371.

Prickett, Alva L., and Mikesell, R. Merrill, *Principles of Accounting,* rev. ed. New York: The Macmillan Co., 1937. Pp. 493-512.

Rorem, C. Rufus, and Kerrigan, Harry D., *Accounting Method,* 3rd ed. New York: McGraw-Hill Book Co., Inc., 1942. Pp. 319-338.

Scovill, Hiram T., and Moyer, C. A., *Fundamentals of Accounting.* Boston: D. C. Heath and Co., 1940.   Pp. 680-686, 701-722.

XV

Advanced Discussion
of Accounts

INVESTMENTS

Companies frequently own stocks and bonds of other companies, and bonds of the United States government and other governmental units. Sometimes stocks and bonds which are readily saleable are held as a liquid investment. In such cases, the investments are intended to supplement the cash and provide income producing assets in place of cash not needed for day-to-day transactions. Investments so held will ordinarily be shown on the balance sheet along with the other current assets, although some accountants prefer to place them in a separate section between current assets and fixed assets.

Stocks and bonds may be held with the intention of retaining them until maturity, or at least for some time. If this is true, the investment will probably be shown on the balance sheet either with the fixed assets or in a separate section between current assets and fixed assets. It may be that stocks and bonds shown as investments will be retained by the company as a matter of business policy. Some investments are held for purposes of control, and others are held for the purpose of maintaining satisfactory business relationships with customers.

In general, it may be stated that the purpose for which an investment is held determines the position of the investment items on the balance sheet. Temporary investments frequently are treated as current assets, and permanent investments as fixed assets, but either one or both kinds of investments may be shown in a separate investments section between current assets and fixed assets.

DISCOUNTS

Cash Discounts. On wholesale transactions a customer is frequently permitted to pay less than the amount of the invoice if payment is made within a stated limited period. Such a deduction is referred to as a cash discount. For example, when the terms of a sale are "2/10, n/30," the customer deducts 2 per cent if he pays the invoice within 10 days of its date, but, if he delays payment, the net or entire amount will be due in 30 days. An enterprise considers cash discounts taken by customers as *sales discounts*, and cash discounts allowed by creditors as *purchase discounts*.

Sales discounts may be shown on the profit and loss statement in the sales, the operating expenses, or the non-operating expenses sections. If sales discounts are in the sales section, they are a deduction from gross sales. If they are in the operating expenses section, they are either a selling expense or a general and administrative expense. If they are in the non-operating expenses section, they are a non-operating expense.

Purchase discounts may be shown on the profit and loss statement in the cost of goods sold section as a deduction from purchases. Sometimes they are shown in the general and administrative expenses division of the operating expenses section as a financial management income offsetting financial management expenses. They may be shown in the non-operating income and expenses section as a non-operating income.

While there is some difference of opinion as to the proper place for sales discounts and purchase discounts on the profit and loss statement, a consistent policy should be followed by a business enterprise.

Trade Discounts. A rather common business procedure is the allowance of a deduction from the catalogue price, or list price, of merchandise to determine the invoice price without reference to the date of payment. Such an allowance is ordinarily termed a *trade discount* and may include allowances made for various reasons. All customers may be given a trade discount, either to conceal the actual price from persons who might see the catalogue, or to avoid rewriting the catalogue. The trade discount can be changed when the price level changes and no new catalogue need be issued. Individual customers can be favored through the granting of trade discounts not given to all customers. This may be done to meet competition, to grant lower prices to affiliated companies, or to provide secret rebates. Trade discounts frequently are allowed on the basis of the quantity of merchandise purchased.

Discount on Notes. Interest collected in advance by banks or others on loans to customers is known as *discount*. The portion of discount on notes payable which is applicable to the current fiscal period will be shown on the profit and loss statement in the interest expense. If part of the discount is not consumed at the close of the fiscal period, such part will ordinarily be shown on the balance sheet as prepaid interest, a deferred charge.

The portion of discount on notes receivable earned during the accounting period is interest income. The unearned portion is interest received in advance, ordinarily a deferred credit to income.

Discount on Bonds. Bonds may be sold for less than face value. This gives rise to a discount on bonds. The issuing corporation considers this as discount on bonds payable, which is a deferred charge to interest expense. The investor purchasing bonds for less than the face value would consider the discount as a discount on bonds receivable, which is a deferred credit to income.

Discount on Capital Stock.   When stock is issued for less than its par value it is said to be issued at a discount. When stock is originally issued at a discount, the discount should be shown on the balance sheet as a deduction from the par value of the stock. When a corporation reacquires its own stock, such stock is known as treasury stock. If treasury stock is acquired for less than the par value, this is considered as a discount on treasury stock and should be considered as a capital surplus account.

CAPITAL AND REVENUE
EXPENDITURES

An expenditure is the payment of money or services or the incurring of debts for any asset or expense. Expenditures are customarily divided into two groups, capital expenditures and revenue expenditures.

A capital expenditure is one which increases the value at which a fixed, or capital, asset may properly be carried on the books.[1]

A revenue expenditure is one which constitutes a proper deduction from income, or revenue.[2] It is an expense.

In distinguishing between capital and revenue expenditures the term *capitalizing* is frequently used. Capitalizing is charging an expenditure to an asset account.

It is essential that the proper distinction be made between capital expenditures and revenue expenditures. If this is not done, the periodic financial statements will be incorrect. If a revenue expenditure is improperly shown as a capital expenditure, expense will be understated, and net profit, assets, and net worth will be overstated. If a capi-

---

1 Capital expenditures sometimes are termed charges to capital, capital charges, or asset expenditures.

2 Revenue expenditures sometimes are termed charges to revenue, charges against revenue, revenue charges, charges to operations, or expense expenditures.

tal expenditure is improperly shown as a revenue expenditure, the opposite will be true: expense will be overstated, and net profit, assets, and net worth will be understated.

CAPITAL GAINS AND LOSSES

Gains and losses which are unusual in occurrence and outside of the regular operations of the enterprise may be considered to be capital gains and losses, or non-operating incomes and expenses. In a corporation such items would affect surplus. They may be shown on an analysis of surplus. Some authorities wish to show these items on the profit and loss statement in the non-operating income and non-operating expense section.

SALES

Sales as previously discussed have included principally the transfer of merchandise for cash or on credit. These two types of sales are the ones generally encountered in sales transactions. There are other common types of sales, however, some of which are: C.O.D. sales, approval sales, installment sales, sales for future delivery, and consignment sales.

Cash Sales. A sale in which the vendor receives the full amount of the sale contract in cash at the time the sale is consummated, is known as a cash sale.

Sales on Credit. Sales on credit are commonly considered to be the transfer of merchandise for which payment will be made at some later date.

C. O. D. Sales. The term C. O. D. is merely an abbreviation for cash, or collect, on delivery. This kind of sale is similar to the cash sale, the difference being that cash is received at the time delivery is made. When delivery is made by the vendor, title passes at time of delivery. When delivery is made by a common carrier, title is usually considered to have passed at the time goods are turned over to the carrier, although possession may not be taken until payment is made.

Approval Sales. When goods are delivered to a customer for his approval, a memorandum record should be made, but title has not passed and a sale should not be recorded until the customer has shown that he will retain the goods.

Installment Sales. This type of sale on credit is one in which the vendor may receive part of the price of the goods at the time the sale is made, and the purchaser agrees to pay the balance at more or less regular intervals over a period of time. There are two principal types of installment sales, one in which title passes at the time of the sale and the vendor has a chattel mortgage for the goods sold, and another in which title does not pass to the purchaser until the merchandise is paid for in full. In an installment sale the vendor may compute his profit as earned: (1) at the time the sale is made, (2) in proportion to the installments received, or (3) at the time the final payment is received.

Sales for Future Delivery. When a sale is made and the merchandise is to be delivered at some future time, profits frequently are not computed until the time delivery is made.

Consignment Sales. Wholesale transactions are sometimes made on the basis that the vendor, who is the consignor, will deliver the goods to the consignee, but the title remains with the consignor until final disposition of the merchandise is made. The consignee sells the goods for the account of the consignor. Such transactions are frequently distinguished from sales, since they are in reality bailments.

ACCOUNTING FOR SALES

In accounting for sales, the procedures vary, and special journals, ledgers, and registers are frequently employed. Although variations are frequent, some general principles may be listed. For a cash sale the entry consists of a debit to Cash and a credit to Sales. For a credit sale, the entry consists of a debit to the individual customer's account, and usually a debit to the Accounts Receivable controlling account, and a credit to Sales. For a C.O.D. sale, a debit may be made to a C.O.D. account and to the Accounts Receivable controlling account, and a credit to Sales. If goods are returned because payment is not received, an entry would be made to debit Sales, and credit the C.O.D. account and the Accounts Receivable controlling account. For installment sales, there are a variety of ways in which the entries are made, some differences being due to the various times in which profits on installment sales are computed. For sales for future delivery, only a memorandum record is necessary prior to delivery of the merchandise. Upon delivery, the entry will be made in accordance with the way in which payment is received. In accounting for consignment sales, it is important that such entries be made as will enable both the consignor and consignee to have a complete picture of the transactions.

ADDITIONAL BIBLIOGRAPHY*

Bolon, Dallas S., *Introduction to Accounting,* 2nd ed. New York: John Wiley & Sons, Inc., 1938. Pp. 429-437.

Cole, Dana F., *Beginning Accounting.* New York: Thomas Y. Crowell Co., 1940. Pp. 315-317, 461-462, 651-655, 692-770.

Elwell, Fayette H., *Elementary Accounting.* Boston: Ginn and Co., 1945. Pp. 169-176, 509-534.

Hatfield, Henry R., Sanders, Thomas H., and Burton, Norman L., *Accounting Principles and Practices.* Boston: Ginn and Co., 1940. Pp. 319-338.

Himmelblau, David, *Principles of Accounting,* rev. ed. New York: The Ronald Press Co., 1934. Pp. 153-162, 175-190.

Howard, Stanley E., *The A B C of Accounting,* 3rd ed. Princeton: Princeton University Press, 1938, Pp. 104-106, 198-220.

Jackson, J. Hugh, *Accounting Principles.* Los Angeles: Charles R. Hadley Co., 1944. Pp. 132-135, 597-638.

---

* For other references, see the QUICK REFERENCE TABLE TO STANDARD TEXTBOOKS in the forepart of this book.

Kelley, Arthur C., *Essentials of Accounting.* New York: American Book Co., 1935. Pp. 97-98, 274-281.

Kennedy, Donald D., Esterly, George R., and von Minden, William J., *Introductory Accounting.* New York: The Ronald Press Co., 1942. Pp. 28-30, 53-57, 340-341.

Lamberton, Robert A., *Fundamentals of Accounting.* New York: Longmans, Green and Co., 1942. Pp. 82-83.

Mason, Perry, *Fundamentals of Accounting,* 2nd ed. Brooklyn: The Foundation Press, Inc., 1947. Pp. 159-166, 172-174, 335-337.

Prickett, Alva L., and Mikesell, R. Merrill, *Principles of Accounting,* rev. ed. New York: The Macmillan Co., 1937. Pp. 267-293.

Rorem, C. Rufus, and Kerrigan, Harry D., *Accounting Method,* 3rd ed. New York: McGraw-Hill Book Co., Inc., 1942. Pp. 113-115, 468-477.

Scovill, Hiram T., and Moyer, C. A., *Fundamentals of Accounting.* Boston: D. C. Heath and Co., 1940. Pp. 115-119, 334-335, 661-701, 729-736.

XVI

Accounting and Management

GROUPS FOR WHOM STATEMENTS ARE PREPARED

The diverse groups interested in a business enterprise do not have precisely the same viewpoint, and therefore the financial statements prepared especially for them will vary in the type and extent of details presented.

1. *Management* is interested in the financial statements, especially a detailed profit and loss statement, in order to secure information needed for efficient operation of the enterprise. The statements should be shown in sufficient detail to enable the managers, through analysis and interpretation, to evaluate past operations and formulate future policies.

2. *Owners* sometimes are managers of small business enterprises, but in corporations, particularly those which are large, owners and managers are usually different individuals. Financial statements prepared for the use of the owners should enable the owners to ascertain the efficiency of the management, their individual equity, and the returns to be expected.

3. *Creditors* are interested in statements which will indicate the ability of the enterprise to meet its obligations at maturity. The short-term creditors are interested in the liquidity of the enterprise, whereas long-term creditors are interested in the ability of the enterprise to make interest payments, as well as its

ability to meet obligations in the more distant future. This is true of both present and prospective creditors.

4. *Investors,* present and prospective, are interested in statements which indicate the security of the investments, as well as the efficiency of the management, in order that they may judge the likelihood that both interest and principal obligations will be met in the future.

5. *Employees* have been given statements, particularly in recent years, which present a readily understandable picture of the operations and condition of the enterprise, and its relationship to the employees. While such statements are not used by all businesses, they are a means of keeping the employees informed and interested in the business. In some cases the employees are also stockholders. This gives them a dual interest in the enterprise.

6. *Governmental agencies* frequently require financial statements for such purposes as taxation and control. The requirements of the Securities and Exchange Commission are an example. The reports and returns so required appear in many forms to which the enterprise must conform.

7. The *public* is interested in the financial statements which indicate the security and stability of such enterprises as banks, insurance companies, and public utilities. The financial statements of a public utility company may assist the public in judging correctness of the rates charged. Financial reports of governmental units should be made available to the public.

ANALYSIS AND INTERPRETATION OF FINANCIAL STATEMENTS

The accounting department prepares analyses and interpretations of financial statements as required by the management. These statements can include information desired by all of the groups mentioned above. The accounting records furnish much of the information upon which the analyses are based. Frequently no interpretation of the statements is attempted by the accounting department, but it is left to the judgment of those who use the statements. In the preparation of an analysis various devices are used, some of which will now be considered.

Percentages. Percentages are used in the analysis of both balance sheets and profit and loss statements. They are employed on the balance sheet so that each percentage listed shows the proportion of a specific asset, or group of assets, to a larger group. The same procedure is followed in connection with both the liabilities and net worth. On the profit and loss statement percentages are used so that each percentage listed shows the proportion of one item, or group of items, to a larger group, or to some base figure such as sales.

Ratios. A ratio indicates the relationship of one number to another. In the analysis of balance sheets and profit and loss statements, a number of ratios are commonly employed, some of which have considerable significance if properly interpreted. Valuable information about trends in an enterprise may be obtained by comparing similar ratios on a series of balance sheets or profit and loss statements. In discussing a ratio, care should be taken to state it correctly. It is computed by dividing the first named item by the second. Following are some of the typical financial statement ratios:

1. Current assets to current liabilities (the current ratio)[1]

---

1 The excess of current assets over current liabilities (net current assets) is called *working capital*. Some accountants prefer to call the net current assets *net working capital*.

2. The total of cash, receivables, and marketable securities to current liabilities (the acid test ratio)

3. Notes receivable to accounts receivable

4. Merchandise to current assets

5. Current assets to total assets

6. Plant and equipment to fixed liabilities

7. Fixed assets to total assets

8. Fixed assets to fixed liabilities

9. Notes payable to accounts payable

10. Total liabilities to total assets

11. Total liabilities to net worth

12. Capital to fixed assets

13. Surplus to net worth

14. Net worth to fixed assets

15. Net worth to total assets

16. Net profit to net sales

17. Cost of goods sold to average merchandise inventory (the merchandise turnover)

18. Net sales to receivables

19. Net sales to fixed assets

20. Net sales to net worth

21. Net profit to net worth

22. Net profit to capital stock

23. Net profit less dividends on preferred stock to common capital stock

24. Net profit to total assets.

Comparative and Cumulative Statements. These statements are used frequently in analyses. Both the balance sheet and the profit and loss statement can be prepared in either comparative or cumulative form. Comparative statements provide a method of comparing the financial statements of one period with similar statements of one or more preceding periods. This is accomplished by showing in one column the figures for the current period, while in one or more other columns will be shown the figures with which comparison is to be made. A separate column is sometimes used to show the amount of increase or decrease, and yet another column to show the percentage increase or decrease.

Cumulative statements usually are interim statements prepared at intervals during a fiscal year. Each statement contains a column to show the figures for the current part of the year, such as one month, and another column to show the cumulative figures for the year to date.

A combination may be used which provides both comparative and cumulative information. In this variation one column is used for the current figures, another column for figures for the same period last year, a third column for the cumulative total to date for this fiscal year, and a fourth column for the cumulative total to this same date for the preceding fiscal year.

Need for Supplementary Statements. Supplementary statements, or supplementary schedules, are prepared particularly for the use of the management. Such statements ordinarily include information in greater detail than is desired on the formal financial statements. Examples are the schedules relating to the balance sheet. A schedule, or abstract, of accounts receivable and of accounts payable, will list the individual accounts remaining on the books at the close of the fiscal period, together with the amounts involved. The totals of such lists will be the same as the amounts shown for accounts receivable and accounts payable on the balance sheet. Other supporting schedules show the detailed information concerning such balance sheet items as notes receivable, notes payable, cash, machinery, and buildings.

In addition to a schedule of bank balances which comprise the cash total, a detailed schedule may provide an analysis and classification of the receipts and disbursements of cash.

An analysis of sales may be prepared to provide a breakdown of the sales figure in various ways. One method shows separately the amounts of sales for cash and on credit. Another method shows an analysis of sales on the basis of the type of commodity sold. A third method shows the geographical distribution of sales.

Other analyses will be prepared to provide additional supplementary statements as desired by the management.

In many cases it is essential that supplementary statements be prepared promptly if the management is to use them in policy determination. The work sheet is an aid to the rapid preparation of financial statements, both formal and supplementary.

INTERNAL CHECKS

A system of internal check provides that the records of each employee must be checked by another employee.

The use of a system of internal check is an aid in the rapid and accurate preparation of the financial statements. Probably the primary purpose of such a system is the prevention of theft of cash and goods, but accompanying benefits are important. An internal check system enables the accounting department to detect and correct errors promptly, frequently prior to the close of the fiscal period. This means that less checking and correcting will need to be done during the time that financial statements and supplementary schedules are being prepared.

BUDGETING

Budgeting provides a practical application of the analysis of financial statements. A budget is a systematic forecast of business operations in financial terms. Such a forecast should be based upon an adequate knowledge of past operations, which is provided by a thorough analysis of the financial statements of an enterprise.

Budgeting is used not only by business enterprises established to earn a profit, but also by non-profit organizations such as churches and governmental units. The increased use of budgetary accounting in recent years has provided management with an important tool for the efficient operation of an enterprise.

The procedure in budgetary accounting is complex, and many variations occur. Nevertheless, some basic principles may be observed. A budget may be prepared for each department in an enterprise, and then a combined budget established for the entire enterprise. The preparation of the budget is usually under the control of an administrative officer who works with the departments in the establishment of departmental budgets in keeping with the desired budget for the entire enterprise. The use of a budget includes the preparation in advance of estimated balance sheets and profit and loss statements. Periodically the estimated financial statements should be compared with the statements showing results of actual operations, in order to assist the management in the formation of business policies.

MACHINE APPLICATIONS IN ACCOUNTING

Many of the accounting activities previously discussed are carried out through the use of mechanical equipment. Ordinarily, special forms are employed in connection with the use of such equipment. These forms are designed to provide the greatest utilization of the equipment for the particular enterprise involved.

Mechanical devices are used in the work of recording, posting, and summarizing, as well as in the preparation of reports.

Advantages of Use. While the advantages of the use of mechanical equipment vary, the following are commonly observed:

1. Speed in operation, and in the preparation of reports

2. Accuracy

3. Neatness

4. More details available

5. Balances and other information readily and continuously available.

Types of Mechanical Equipment. Machines used in the accounting process include typewriters, adding and calculating machines (either key driven or crank driven), cash registers, and punched card tabulating and other electronic equipment. Other machines which are used in a supplementary capacity include the check writer, check cutter and stacker, check protecting device, duplicator, addresser, time recorder, counter, coin changer, and teletypewriter.

INSOLVENCY

When an enterprise is unable to meet its obligations, it is insolvent. It is possible for an insolvent enterprise to continue to operate.

The actions necessary to have a court declare an insolvent enterprise bankrupt can be voluntary or by action of the creditors. Liquidation of a bankrupt concern must proceed under strict court supervision.

A *statement of affairs* is an accounting statement somewhat similar to a balance sheet, prepared to indicate what the creditors can expect to receive from the liquidation of the business. This statement differs from the balance sheet particularly in the method of valuing the items and in the order of their presentation. The assets are usually classified as those assets which are fully pledged, partly pledged, and unpledged. The liabilities are then classified as those liabilities which are preferred, fully secured, partly secured, unsecured, and contingent. The statement of affairs ordinarily shows not only the book value of the assets, but also the amount expected to be realized from the assets.

The statement of affairs is customarily accompanied by a deficiency account, which is supplementary and which shows how the deficiency that has been shown on the statement of affairs arises.

VOCATIONAL AND PROFESSIONAL ASPECTS

Accounting Work Classified. Those who engage in accounting activity are usually classified into the following principal groups: bookkeeper, accountant, auditor, cost accountant, chief accountant, public accountant, and certified public accountant.

Representative Accounting Organizations. Probably the best known accounting organizations in the United States are the American Institute of Certified Public Accountants, state societies of certified public accountants, American Accounting Association, and National Association of Cost Accountants.

Accounting Literature. Current accounting literature of the United States includes the following publications: *Journal of Accountancy*, published by the American Institute of Certified Public Accountants; *Accounting Review*, published by the American Accounting Association; *N. A. C. A. Bulletin*, published by the National Association of Cost Accountants; and *Accountants' Digest*, privately published.

ADDITIONAL BIBLIOGRAPHY*

Bolon, Dallas S., *Introduction to Accounting*, 2nd ed. New York: John Wiley & Sons, Inc., 1938. Pp. 273-275, 370-371, 458-482.

Cole, Dana F., *Beginning Accounting*. New York: Thomas Y. Crowell Co., 1940. Pp. 397-425, 444-449, 625-637.

Elwell, Fayette H., *Elementary Accounting*. Boston: Ginn and Co., 1945. Pp. 579-623.

Hatfield, Henry R., Sanders, Thomas H. and Burton, Norman L., *Accounting Principles and Practices*. Boston: Ginn and Co., 1940. Pp. 335-398, 423-450.

Himmelblau, David, *Principles of Accounting*, rev ed. New York: The Ronald Press Co., 1934. Pp. 191-203.

Howard, Stanley E., *The A B C of Accounting*, 3rd ed. Princeton: Princeton University Press, 1938. Pp. 262-270.

Jackson, J. Hugh, *Accounting Principles*. Los Angeles: Charles R. Hadley Co., 1944. Pp. 349-354, 743-762.

Kelley, Arthur C., *Essentials of Accounting*. New York: American Book Co., 1935. Pp. 356-411.

Kennedy, Donald D., Esterly, George R., and von Minden, William J., *Introductory Accounting*. New York: The Ronald Press Co., 1942. Pp. 114-191, 445-466, 602-664.

Lamberton, Robert A., *Fundamentals of Accounting*. New York: Longmans, Green and Co., 1942. Pp. 425-450.

Rorem, C. Rufus, and Kerrigan, Harry D., *Accounting Method*, 3rd ed. New York: McGraw-Hill Book Co., Inc., 1942. Pp. 559-610, 627-639.

Scovill, Hiram T., and Moyer, C. A., *Fundamentals of Accounting*. Boston: D. C. Heath and Co., 1940. Pp. 485-486, 625-660, 736-738.

* For other references, see the QUICK REFERENCE TABLE TO STANDARD TEXTBOOKS in the forepart of this book.

Appendix A: Illustrative Material

Appendix A: *Illustrative Material*

Material presented here will help the reader to apply and review some of the principles discussed elsewhere in the *Outline*. Numbers in parentheses indicate the pages on which related material appears.

Chart of Accounts

An illustration of a numerical chart of accounts follows these comments. Such a chart is helpful to the bookkeeper and the accountant (34-38), and it may be indispensable if a machine accounting method is used which requires reference to the accounts by number (182-183). Many variations occur. Every chart of accounts should be planned so that it will meet the requirements of the specific company that adopts it.

In the illustrative chart, the principal groups of accounts begin with numbers as follows: assets, 1; liabilities, 2; proprietorship, 3; summary, 4; operating income, 5; operating expense, 6; and non-operating income and non-operating expense, 7. Account numbers within each group begin with the number assigned to that group. For example, under this plan numbers can be assigned as follows:

1   Assets
11   Current assets
    111   Cash
        111.1   Petty cash
        111.2   Cash in bank
    112   Receivables
        112.1   Notes receivable
        112.2   Accounts receivable
            112.21   Accounts receivable, customers
            112.22   Accounts receivable, others
        112V   Reserve for bad debts (a valuation account)

It is not necessary to list the numbers of group captions in a chart of accounts, although some accountants prefer to do so. The following chart shows the numbers of actual accounts only.

A MANUFACTURING COMPANY
CHART OF ACCOUNTS

Current assets: (10)

111.1	Petty cash	(100-101)
111.2	Cash in bank	
112.11	Notes receivable, customers	
112.12	Notes receivable, others	
112.1V	Notes receivable discounted	
112.13	Accrued interest receivable	(65)
112.21	Accounts receivable, customers	
112.22	Accounts receivable, others	
112.23	Loans to employees	
112V	Reserve for doubtful notes and accounts	(71-72)
113.1	Inventories of raw materials	(152)
113.2	Inventories of goods in process	
113.3	Inventories of finished goods	
114.1	Prepaid interest expense	(10-11)
114.2	Prepaid insurance	(66)
114.3	Prepaid taxes and licenses	
114.4	Supplies on hand	(66)
115	Temporary investments	(168-169)

Fixed assets: (11, 156)

121	Land	
122.1	Building, factory	
122.2	Building, office	
122V	Reserve for depreciation of buildings	(73, 146)
123	Machinery and equipment	
123V	Reserve for depreciation of machinery and equipment	
124	Furniture and fixtures	
124V	Reserve for depreciation of furniture and fixtures	

125   Patterns and drawings

125V   Reserve for depreciation of patterns and drawings

Other assets: (11)

131.1   Investments in affiliated companies   (168-169)

131.2   Other permanent investments

132   Sinking fund in hands of trustee   (148)

133.1   Goodwill   (154)

133.2   Patents

133.2V Reserve for amortization of patents

134   Unamortized discount on bonds payable
                                       (139,170)

135   Organization expense   (121)

Current liabilities: (11)

211.1   Notes payable, banks

211.2   Notes payable, others

212   Accounts payable, trade creditors

213.1   Accrued wages payable

213.2   Accrued interest payable   (65)

213.3   Accrued payroll taxes

213.4   Accrued income taxes

213.5   Other accrued expenses

214.1   Deferred rent income

214.2   Other deferred income

215   Advances from stockholders, officers, and employees

216   Dividends payable   (131-133)

217   Other current liabilities

Fixed liabilities:

221   Mortgages payable

221.1   Bonds payable   (135-145)

222.2   Unamortized premium on bonds payable (139)

223   Other long-term liabilities

Capital stock:

311	Capital stock, preferred	(122-123)
311V	Treasury stock, preferred	(128)
312	Capital stock, common	

Surplus:

321.1	Paid-in surplus	(128-130)
321.2	Donated surplus	(130)
321.3	Revaluation surplus	(130)
322.12	Reserve for plant extension	(147)
322.13	Reserve for contingencies	(147)
322.2	Retained earnings (or earned surplus) unappropriated	(130)

Summary:

410	Profit and loss account	(131)

Operating income: (18-19)

511	Sales, home office	
511V	Sales returns and allowances, home office	
512	Sales, branch office	(159)

Manufacturing costs   (151-153)

611.1	Purchases of raw materials
611.1V	Purchases returns and allowances
611.21	Salaries and wages, purchasing department
611.22	Heat and light, purchasing department
611.23	Telephone and telegraph, purchasing department
611.24	Depreciation of purchasing department equipment
611.25	Miscellaneous purchasing department expenses
611.3	Receiving department expenses
611.4	Freight, express, and cartage, inward
611.51	Direct labor, production department 1

611.52	Direct labor, production department 2	
612.1	Indirect labor	(153)
612.2	Factory heat, light, power, and water	
612.3	Factory insurance	
612.41	Repairs and maintenance of factory building	
612.42	Repairs and maintenance of machinery	
612.51	Depreciation of factory building	
612.52	Depreciation of factory equipment	
612.6	Factory supplies used	
612.7	Royalties	
612.8	Taxes	
612.9	Sundry factory expenses	

Selling expenses: (20)

621.1	Salaries and commissions, salesmen	
621.2	Salaries and commissions, sales supervision	
621.3	Clerical salaries, sales deparment	
622	Traveling expenses, salesmen	
623	Advertising and samples	
624	Repairs and maintenance of sales equipment	
625	Depreciation of sales equipment	
626	Sales department supplies used	
627	Freight outward	
628	Bad debts	(71)
629	Sundry selling expenses	

General and administrative expenses: (21)

631.1	Officers' salaries	
631.2	Directors' fees	
631.3	Office salaries	
631.4	Legal and accounting fees	
632	Traveling expenses, general	
633	Repairs and maintenance of general office equipment	
634	Depreciation of general office equipment	
635.1	Printing and stationery, general office	
635.2	General office supplies used	

635.3	Postage and express, general	
636	Telephone and telegraph	
637	Insurance, general	
638	Taxes and licenses, general	
639	Sundry administrative expenses	

Non-operating income: (21)

711	Interest earned	
712	Dividends received	
713	Rent income	
721	Purchase discounts	(169)
731	Sales of scrap	
741	Miscellaneous non-operating income	(172)

Non-operating expenses: (21)

761	Taxes on investment property	
771	Interest expense	(65)
772	Sales discounts	(169)
781	Miscellaneous non-operating expenses	

Financial Statements

Sample forms for a balance sheet and an income statement of a mercantile concern appear on the following three pages. It will be noted that the items on the forms are similar to many of the items listed on the manufacturing company chart of accounts. The principal differences result from the fact that the mercantile firm has only one merchandise inventory instead of three, and it has no manufacturing accounts.

Supplementary schedules can be used to supply information in addition to that shown on the balance sheet and the income statement (155-157).

A MERCANTILE
BALANCE
December

ASSETS

CURRENT ASSETS:

Cash on hand and in banks..
Notes and accounts receivable:
  Notes receivable, customers.....................................
  Accounts receivable, customers
  Other receivables (details)...
  Less: Reserve for bad debts......................................
Merchandise inventory (state basis)...............................
Prepaid expenses (interest, insurance, taxes, supplies, etc.).............
        Total current assets...

FIXED ASSETS:

Land...
Buildings...
  Less: Reserve for depreciation of buildings........................
Furniture and fixtures...
  Less: Reserve for depreciation of furniture and fixtures..............
Delivery equipment..
  Less: Reserve for depreciation of delivery equipment...............
Other fixed assets (details)..
  Less: Reserve for depreciation....................................
        Total fixed assets..

OTHER ASSETS:

Intangibles (details)..
Miscellaneous (details)..

TOTAL ASSETS...

COMPANY
SHEET
31, 19..

LIABILITIES

CURRENT LIABILITIES:

Notes payable...
Accounts payable, trade creditors..................................
Accrued expenses (wages, interest, taxes, etc.)......................
Other current liabilities (details)..................................
      Total current liabilities.....................................

FIXED LIABILITIES:

Mortgages payable..
Other long-term liabilities (details)...............................
      Total fixed liabilities.......................................
      Total liabilities..

PROPRIETORSHIP

OWNER'S NAME:

Investment at beginning of year...................................
Add: Additional investment during year..........................
       Net profit for the year......................................
Deduct: Withdrawals..
Total proprietorship at end of year................................

TOTAL LIABILITIES AND PROPRIETORSHIP...................

A MERCANTILE COMPANY
PROFIT AND LOSS STATEMENT

For the year ending December 31, 19.....

INCOME FROM SALES:

Gross sales...
Less: Sales returns and allowances..................................
    Net sales..

COST OF GOODS SOLD:

Merchandise inventory at beginning of year.........................
Purchases and freight in...
Less: Purchases returns and allowances............................
       Cost of merchandise available for sale........................
Less: Merchandise inventory at end of year.........................
       Cost of goods sold..

GROSS PROFIT...

OPERATING EXPENSES:

Selling expenses:
    Sales salaries and commissions....................................
    Advertising..
    List other .selling expenses (delivery expense, insurance on sales
       equipment and merchandise, depreciation of sales equipment, bad
       debts, sales supplies used, etc.)...............................
       Total selling expenses......................................
General and administrative expenses:
    Office salaries...
    List other general expenses (rent, telephone, light, heat, taxes,
       insurance, depreciation, office supplies used, etc.).................
       Total general and administrative expenses....................

       Total operating expenses....................................

NET OPERATING PROFIT..

NON-OPERATING INCOME AND EXPENSES:

Non-operating income (interest, rent, purchase discounts, etc.).........
Non-operating expenses (interest, sales discount, etc.).................

NET PROFIT..

Appendix B: Sample Examination Questions

Appendix B: Sample Examination Questions and Answers

Sample questions taken from accounting examinations may be useful to the reader in reviewing his accounting knowledge. There are two principal kinds of questions in an accounting examination. They are the essay or discussion type and the objective or short-answer type.

The first group of questions (Part 1) consists of the essay or discussion type. No answers are given, but each question is followed by figures in parentheses referring to the page or pages in the *Outline* on which an answer to the question can be found. The remaining groups (Part 2) consist of the objective or short-answer type of questions. Answers and references to pages in this *Outline* are indicated for these questions on p. 209.

Part 1

Instructions. Answer the questions in the following group fully, but do not use more words than necessary. Be sure that each answer indicates your understanding of the material covered.

1. (a) Define the terms *bookkeeping* and *accounting*, and indicate how they differ. (1-2)

   (b) What is the primary purpose of accounting? (3)

2. List the classes of assets and liabilities, and describe each class briefly. (10-12)

3. (a) Describe a profit and loss statement. (16-18)

   (b) Give a brief description of each of the items that make up the cost of goods sold section of a profit and loss statement. (19-20)

4. (a) Prepare a T account for each of five classes of accounts, and, with the help of plus and minus signs, show which side of each account is used for increases and which side for decreases. (27)

(b) What is meant by the financial statement sequence of accounts in the ledger? (34)

(c) Explain one method of preparing a trial balance of ledger accounts. (39-40)

5. (a) Describe the processes of journalizing and of posting. (46-49)

(b) Explain the relationship between the journal and the ledger. (49)

6. (a) How does the accrual basis of accounting differ from the cash basis? (51-52)

(b) List the steps in the accounting cycle. (59)

(c) Define *depreciation*, and explain one method of computing it. (67-70)

7. (a) List the advantages of special journals. (82-83)

(b) How can a subsidiary ledger be converted into a self-balancing ledger? (86-87)

8. (a) Discuss the importance of business papers. (96)

(b) Why should a bank reconciliation be prepared? (99-100)

9. Is the voucher register a journal or a ledger? Explain briefly. (105-107)

10. (a) Describe the proprietary accounts for a single proprietorship and for a partnership. (110-115)

(b) Discuss the distribution of partnership profits and losses. (115-116)

11. (a) What journal entries are made to record sales by a corporation of its own previously unissued stock? (124-126)

(b) What disposition is made of a corporation's profit or loss at the close of an accounting period? (131)

12. (a) How do nominal and effective interest rates affect the price of bonds? (138-139)

(b) Where should reserves be placed on a company's balance sheet?   (146-147)

13. How do the financial statements reveal whether an enterprise is a manufacturing or a mercantile concern?   (151-157)

14. Discuss the preparation of financial statements for an enterprise with branches.   (163)

15. Name five kinds of discount, and discuss one of them briefly.   (169-171)

16. How are percentages and ratios used in the analysis of financial statements?   (177-179)

Part 2

I. Instructions.   In each of the following statements, select from the answers given the one which *best* answers or completes the statement.   More than one answer may apply, but one answer will be the best.   Indicate your choice by underscoring the number of the answer.

1. Cash appears on the financial statements as:
    1. An asset
    2. A proprietary account
    3. A current asset
    4. A reserve account
    5. A surplus account

2. By gross profit we mean:
    1. Sales minus cost of goods sold
    2. Sales minus net profit on sales
    3. Gross margin minus cost of goods sold
    4. Gross trading profit minus operating expenses
    5. Sales minus selling expenses

3. Which of the following would require a debit entry?
    1. Increase in an income account
    2. Increase in a proprietorship account
    3. Increase in a liability account
    4. Increase in an asset account

4. A statement showing the items which make up the difference between the bank statement and the cash account is known as:

   1. An adjustment sheet
   2. A reconciliation of bank balance
   3. An income statement
   4. A statement of surplus

5. Company X capital stock having a par value of $1,000 is donated to Company X. The proper entry is:

   1. Debit capital stock, credit donated surplus
   2. Debit donated surplus, credit treasury stock
   3. Debit treasury stock, credit donated surplus
   4. Debit capital stock, credit earned surplus
   5. Debit treasury stock, credit paid-in surplus

6. Stock referred to above was reissued at $1,200. The proper entry is:

   1. Debit cash and donated surplus, credit treasury stock
   2. Debit cash, credit treasury stock and donated surplus
   3. Debit cash, credit treasury stock
   4. Debit cash, credit treasury stock and earned surplus
   5. Debit cash and earned surplus, credit treasury stock

7. A promise under seal to pay a definite sum of money at a stated time and to pay interest at a stipulated rate is known as:

   1. A preferred stock
   2. A promissory note
   3. A mortgage payable
   4. A bond
   5. A common stock

8. Periodic amortization of premium on bonds payable requires adjustment of:

    1. Earned surplus
    2. Capital surplus
    3. Reserve for sinking fund
    4. Interest income
    5. Interest expense

9. The purpose of a reserve for bond sinking fund is:

    1. To set aside cash for payment of the bonds at maturity
    2. To provide for payment of interest on the bonds
    3. To serve as a valuation reserve
    4. To retain earnings and provide more security for the bonds
    5. To increase the proprietorship total on the balance sheet

10. The *current ratio* is the ratio of:

    1. Net sales to net profit
    2. Net sales to proprietorship
    3. Current assets to current liabilities
    4. Current assets to total assets
    5. Current liabilities to current assets

II. Instructions. Statements in this section are either true or false. If a statement is true, place a plus sign to the left of the number of the statement. If it is false, place a zero to the left of the number of the statement.

1. Accounting involves the recording of business transactions in monetary terms.

2. Posting is done by making entries in the journal.

3. It is desirable to record loss from bad debts before ascertaining definitely which specific accounts will be uncollectible.

4. Use of special journals retards the division of labor, making it difficult to distribute the work among the bookkeepers.

5. When a voucher register is used, a purchases journal and an accounts payable ledger are no longer necessary.

6. C, who purchased a 25 per cent interest in a partnership composed of A and B, is entitled to 25 per cent of the firm's profits in the absence of any agreement relating to the distribution of profits.

7. Market value of stock can be computed from the information shown on the balance sheet.

8. A debit balance in an overhead account indicates that overhead was underabsorbed.

9. The debit balance in one reciprocal account must equal the credit balance in the other.

10. The expression 2/10, n/30, means that a discount of 2 per cent is to be granted if payment is made within 30 days.

III. Instructions. Indicate by a plus sign, each answer which is correct, and by a zero, each answer which is wrong. Place the marks to the left of the questions.

1. A purpose of the closing entries is:

   a. To facilitate posting and taking the trial balance

   b. To close the nominal accounts so that they may be used to accumulate only the costs or revenue of the future

    c. To balance the suspense accounts so that they may be used to accumulate only the costs or revenue of the future

    d. To transfer the net result of the period from the expense and income accounts to a proprietorship account

2. Profit for the year would be overstated if adjusting entries were omitted for:

    a. Accrued wages payable

    b. Interest accrued on notes receivable

    c. Depreciation

    d. Accrued taxes payable

    e. Bad debts

IV. Instructions. Several books of original entry are listed below, each of which is designated by one or two letters. Following them is a series of transactions. At the left of the number of each transaction, write the letter or letters indicating the journal in which the transaction should ordinarily be recorded. This is not a complete list of transactions of the business.

Books of original entry:

    CD   Cash disbursements journal
    CR   Cash receipts journal
    J   General journal
    P   Purchases journal
    S   Sales journal

Transactions:

    1. J. J. Jones invested cash in the television business.

    2. Purchased television sets, radios, and **records** from R. T. Smith on account. Terms, 2/10, n/30.

3. Purchased an adding machine for cash.

4. Paid rent for the month.

5. Sold phonograph records to L. Perry on account.

6. Returned some poor quality merchandise to R. T. Smith for credit.

7. Issued a note to R. T. Smith in payment of his account.

8. Withdraw a small amount of cash for personal use.

9. Adjusted the merchandise inventory account.

10. Closed the profit and loss summary account.

Answers to Part 2

I

Ques.	Ans.	Text Ref.	Ques.	Ans.	Text Ref.
1	3	10	6	2	129
2	1	20	7	4	135
3	4	28	8	5	140
4	2	99-100	9	4	147
5	3	129	10	3	178-179

II

Ques.	Ans.	Text Ref.	Ques.	Ans.	Text Ref.
1	+	1	6	0	115
2	0	48	7	0	124
3	+	71	8	+	153
4	0	87	9	+	162
5	+	105-107	10	0	169

III

Ques.	Ans.	Text Ref.	Ques.	Ans.	Text Ref.
1a	0	57	2a	+	65-72
1b	+	57	2b	0	65-72
1c	0	57	2c	+	65-72
1d	+	57	2d	+	65-72
			2e	+	65-72

IV

Text Reference: pp. 79-93

Ques.	Ans.	Ques.	Ans.	Ques.	Ans.
1	CR	4	CD	8	CD
2	P	5	S	9	J
3	CD	6	J	10	J
		7	J		

Index